A HISTORY OF
WRESTLING
IN IOWA
GROWING GOLD

DAN McCOOL

Published by The History Press
Charleston, SC
www.historypress.com

Copyright © 2019 by Daniel McCool
All rights reserved

Harold Nichols photo on front cover courtesy of Iowa State University; Jim Miller photo on front cover courtesy of Wartburg College. Photos of Dan Gable, Tom Brands, Nick Mitchell and Chuck Patten by Dan McCool.

First published 2019

Manufactured in the United States

ISBN 9781467142984

Library of Congress Control Number: 2019950036

Notice: The information in this book is true and complete to the best of our knowledge. It is offered without guarantee on the part of the author or The History Press. The author and The History Press disclaim all liability in connection with the use of this book.

All rights reserved. No part of this book may be reproduced or transmitted in any form whatsoever without prior written permission from the publisher except in the case of brief quotations embodied in critical articles and reviews.

CONTENTS

Acknowledgements 5
Introduction: Wrestling and Iowa 7

1. Frank Gotch 11
2. Iowa's Olympic Gold 23
3. University of Iowa 32
4. Iowa State 45
5. Northern Iowa 58
6. Wartburg 71
7. Grand View 84
8. Junior College 98
9. Waverly–Shell Rock's Record 112
10. Girls' Wrestling 136
11. The Maleceks 155
12. The Other Side 163

Bibliography 173
About the Author 175

ACKNOWLEDGEMENTS

Thank you to Chad Rhoad for giving me the opportunity to do this book. I hope you enjoy the finished product, good sir. Special thanks to the wrestlers who have allowed me to document their efforts for years. Thank you to Diane for putting up with me during the writing process and for your wonderful technical and design skills. Without you, I'm lost in the woods. Additional thanks go to Mike Chapman for being a role model in writing books as well as for being patient and helping with historical knowledge. Kudos to Dan Gable, Tom Brands, Barry Davis, Pete Bush, Ed Banach, Pete Galea, Bob Antonacci, Chuck Patten, Don Briggs, Keith Poolman, Jim Miller, Joe Breitbach, Eric Keller, Nick Mitchell, Troy Plummer, Kent Henning, Joe Hatchett, Doug Trees, Dennie Friederichs, Al Frost, Eric Thompson, Cody Caldwell, Jason Christenson, Chris Krueger, Jim Duschen, Charlotte Bailey, Lewie Curtis, Jean Berger, Alan Beste, Atina Bibbs, Megan Black, Felicity Taylor, Rachel Watters, brothers Joe, Dennis and Dave Malecek, Jan George, Doug Manley, Clint Koedam, Adam Allard, John Henrich and the Gerbracht family—especially Ali, Chad and Tonya—for giving of your time to help tell a story. Thank you to Frosty for the frequent naps, which allowed me to write.

INTRODUCTION

WRESTLING AND IOWA

If there is such a thing as an indigenous sport to a state, wrestling would be Iowa's choice. No other sport mirrors the agriculture-based life of so much of the population and offers a singular reward like wrestling does. The season begins full of hope, much like spring planting of crops. The harvest is in February for high school wrestlers and in March for the college, but only 6 percent of the 672 wrestlers in the three-class high school state tournament will weather all obstacles and bring home gold. The numbers get smaller in college. As many as 330 athletes contend for ten gold medals, and only 3 percent have a winning harvest.

Lewie Curtis, wrestling coordinator for the Iowa High School Athletic Association, said the sport and the farm fit like a hand in a chore glove.

"It's a cornerstone or a foundation for so many people in Iowa, I think, that they do go hand in hand. I think, too, wrestling is a sport that is all about getting your hands on things, pushing and pulling and manhandling things," Curtis said. "If you're a farmer, you've got to do the same thing, whether it's cattle or pigs or turkeys or whatever livestock you're raising, or if it's just shoveling, moving things and pushing things around. That old-school way of doing things just lends itself to the sport too."

Those who did not get the biggest, best harvest have to figuratively dust themselves off and prepare for the next season, much like a farmer who loses one year's crop to flooding, drought or hail orders the fertilizer and seeds for the coming season.

Introduction

"The sport and the way of life are very similar in that regard as well. The interesting part of it is when you're a farmer, that's what you are. You just do it and you keep coming back. You might lose money, you go do it again, you try to do it better till you make money, till you can expand and do more with what you have, or you become satisfied with what you have and you're glad to have it," Curtis said. "I think with wrestling it's similar in that you can put the time and effort in, you hope things go the right way for you and, if they do, you can reap some rewards. If they don't, you have a choice to make—either stick with it or you bail out. They don't bail out. The farm kids don't bail out, that's for sure."

Norman Borlaug of Cresco placed third in the 1932 state wrestling tournament. Borlaug was awarded the Nobel Peace Prize in 1970 for his work in developing a variety of wheat that was resistant to drought and blight, and he has been credited with preventing the starvation of over one billion people. *Courtesy of Cresco Public Library.*

Even the cherished location of the state tournament fit the motif well. Veterans Memorial Auditorium in Des Moines played host to the tournament in 1970 and then from 1972 to 2005. Its moniker? "The Barn." It was cavernous inside, with enough space for eight wrestling mats and thousands of people, many of whom kept a perpetual walking ring around the mats as they followed their wrestlers. The balcony seating was like a hayloft—off the floor but not too far from the action. The place seemed a little dusty, but no one's allergies seemed to kick up. Ed Winger of Urbandale was the public address voice of the event, and he stirred the wrestlers and the crowd with his "Wrestlers, clear the mats. Wrestlers, let's clear the mats please" call minutes prior to the start of each session.

"Everybody wanted your name announced at Vets Auditorium on Saturday night, right? That was the ultimate goal," said Dennis Malecek, one of three brothers from Osage who learned to work on a farm and competed at state in Vets.

Iowa's pride in wrestling shows through in its success:

- Iowa is the first state to have a national champion team in NCAA Division I, Division II, Division III, NAIA and Junior College.

Introduction

- Four schools—Iowa State, Iowa State Teachers College (which later became University of Northern Iowa), Cornell College and Iowa—have won the NCAA Division I team title. That's the most from any state.
- Going into the 2019–20 season, there have been 204 individuals who graduated from Iowa high schools and won a total of 261 national championships in the five divisions: NCAA Division I, Division II, Division III, NAIA and Junior College. Ralph Lupton of Toledo was the first in 1928; Drew Foster of Mediapolis was the most recent in 2019.
- Success went international as five products of Iowa's schools won gold medals in the Summer Olympics. They are Allie Morrison (Marshalltown, 1928 Amsterdam), Glen Brand (Clarion, 1948 London), Bill Smith (Council Bluffs Jefferson, 1952 Helsinki), Dan Gable (Waterloo West, 1972 Munich) and Tom Brands (Sheldon, 1996 Atlanta). Five others earned either silver or bronze medals: Nat Pendleton (Davenport, 1920 Antwerp, second at heavyweight); Lloyd Appleton (Edgewood, 1928 Amsterdam, second at 158.5); Gerald Leeman (Osage, 1948 London, second at 125.5); Barry Davis (Cedar Rapids Prairie, 1984 Los Angeles, second at 125.5) and Terry Brands (Sheldon, 2000 Sydney, third at 127.75).

The IHSAA's Curtis grew up the son of a wrestling coach. He became a second-generation coach and led Underwood to a pair of team championships at Vets. He's seen the correlation between farm work and being a champion wrestler: "The No. 1 thing is it's hard work, and if you're going to be good at it, you don't have any choice. You've got to work hard at it. It's from sunup to sundown and sometimes beyond that. There's very few, if any, days off. And then, in addition to that for those directly involved in it, there's also those people that are indirectly involved in it that just do nothing but support you and buy into what you're doing. The farmer's wife who is hauling food out to him in the field and doing all the stuff they have to do to keep the farmstead running. If they had to rely on the husband to be there doing all that, it wouldn't work. So they're pulling their weight, not unlike the parents of the wrestler or the brothers and sisters of the wrestler who are hauling them around, going to their meets or making sure they're eating properly, giving them no excuses to fail. I think all of those things combined, that's what I like about it."

Introduction

Wrestling is considered a winter sport, but it also has good fundraising opportunities. During the annual "Grump Days" celebration in Readlyn, a team of adults representing Wapsie Valley High School tangled on an outdoor mat against a group representing Jesup High School. The revenue from that, plus auctioning off members of Wapsie Valley's youth club for an hour or hours of work, benefitted Wapsie's youth club. *Photo by Dan McCool.*

It became easy for Curtis to guess where a wrestler lived.

"I can remember when my dad coached, and he had a lot of kids that were farm kids. It wasn't hard to pick them out. They were the ones who had a little bit bigger arms and shoulders than everybody else," Curtis said. "They had a quiet demeanor about them and a quiet confidence about them.... They didn't say much; they didn't have to. They just went out and did their work on the mat and you didn't hear a lot from them. They just outworked you and a lot of times took you to the woodshed right then and there."

There are more stories from Iowans and the sport of wrestling than there are pages here, but rest assured an entire collection of memories would make any best-seller list. The works likely would cost more than what a farmer gets for a bushel of corn or soybeans, but folks will read the prose every year—about the time to start growing more gold in Iowa.

1
FRANK GOTCH

Mike Chapman of Waterloo, Iowa, became hooked on Frank Gotch at Christmas, back in 1954. A man who talked and wrote about heroes and superstars and great Americans found his *nonpareil*, and that ideal had been deceased for nearly forty years. Time may have reduced the memory of the man for many, but the Gotch name and image refuse to go away. A visit to Gotch's hometown of Humboldt will remind one of the imprint he made and the community's pride in how the world heavyweight champion wrestler never forgot his roots, even when his name was spoken worldwide.

His devotion to home is evident on a statue of Gotch that stands in Bicknell Park, which serves as part of the western edge of downtown Humboldt. At the dawn of the twentieth century, it was a training camp site for Gotch: "I was born an Iowa farm boy, I was raised an Iowa farm boy and I'll die an Iowa farm boy."

If a trip is out of the question, meet Chapman, a U.S. Navy veteran; newspaper man; wrestling historian; creator of a wrestling museum, a wrestling publication and a college award named for Oklahoma three-time NCAA champion Dan Hodge; author of thirty books and arguably the source authority of all things Gotch.

"When I was ten years old, my grandfather Joe Chapman gave me this book, *100 Greatest Sports Heroes*. And I'm reading through it and I come to this page....George Gipp is on one side, Frank Gotch, king of wrestlers, is on the other side," Mike said as he flipped through the book he still

Frank Gotch of Humboldt was arguably the top athlete of the early twentieth century. He won the world heavyweight wrestling championship but never forgot his Iowa roots. A bronze statue of Gotch was placed in the downtown Humboldt park where Gotch used to hold training camp. *Photo by Dan McCool.*

cherishes. "On a farm near the little town of Humboldt, Iowa, a young and handsome giant named Frank Gotch worked long and weary hours trying to scratch a living from the soil. One day, he heard that it was possible to earn a little money as a professional wrestler."

"From then on, they talk about his incredible career and the writer says, 'As the idol of millions in the United States, Canada and Mexico, Gotch made wrestling a big-time sport in his day. As a matter of fact, he drew larger audiences than did the heavyweight champion of boxing when defending his title. By the time Frank was ready to return to his farm, he'd earned about a half-million dollars, a great fortune in those days. Added to that were the honors that Gotch had won over the years. Babies had been named in his honor, as had buildings, toys…and a thousand other things. The word Gotch was a synonym for quality and strength.'"

Chapman said he admired athletes such as Jim Thorpe and Jack Dempsey as a boy. Then came Gotch.

"It all goes back to this Christmas gift I got from my grandpa when I was ten years old. That story changed my life, *Frank Gotch: King of Wrestlers*' and I found out that he grew up in Iowa," Chapman said. "From that moment on, he was my No. 1 sports hero. I'd always been a Jim Thorpe fan. But to me, Gotch was bigger than Jim Thorpe or Jack Dempsey, who I met when I was ten years old. Got his autograph in Waterloo. Bigger than Mickey Mantle, who I was a big fan of. Bigger than Johnny Unitas. Frank Gotch was it for me. It's the spirit of Frank Gotch and Farmer Burns and it's pretty well faded, but this one article—and that's how important reading is—changed my life."

There had been champions before Gotch, most notably Martin "Farmer" Burns, a gentleman from a speck of eastern Iowa called Big Rock. His physical strength and mental fortitude belied his roughly 160-to-170-pound frame. Burns beat Gotch when Gotch was very green and learning the ropes but also helped develop the young man's raw skill into the prowess of a polished athlete who beat George Hackenschmidt, billed as the "Russian Lion," for the world heavyweight championship in 1908 and again in 1911, both times in Chicago. The second match, which drew thirty thousand fans to Comiskey Park, was front-page news throughout the country. Because of his victory, Gotch became arguably the best-known athlete of his time in the country. He endorsed various products and even starred in a play that toured the East Coast and Europe. Gotch also received an invitation from President Theodore Roosevelt to visit the White House.

"I say the spirit of Gotch has lingered over the state of Iowa for decades," Chapman said.

Tom Brands of Sheldon, a three-time NCAA champion at Iowa and a 1996 Olympic gold medalist, said Gotch exemplified the "you-only-get-what-you-earn" comments that Brands has become known for as a coach.

"When I think of Frank Gotch, I think of Iowa farm dirt, I think of blue-collar work ethic and I think of a guy who could scrap with the best of them and did and won," said Brands, wrestling coach at Iowa. "You talk about pain, he won grueling matches where you had to overcome more than just fatigue. You had to overcome severe dehydration in these long bouts. He was Tom Brady in his day, that's how big wrestling was, and he was from Humboldt, Iowa."

The April 4, 1908 *Chicago Tribune* had George Siler's account of the Gotch-Hackenschmidt match, leading with, "Frank Gotch, the greatest wrestler America has ever produced, last night relegated George Hackenschmidt, the 'Russian Lion,' to the ranks by forcing him to quit at the end of what probably was the most desperate mat battle in the history of wrestling."

The scheduled best-of-three-falls match, witnessed by a crowd listed at six thousand and including legendary football coach Amos Alonzo Stagg, lasted just over two hours, ending at 12:30 a.m. Back home, the *Humboldt Independent* published a 2:00 a.m. "extra" edition with the front page blaring "FRANK A. GOTCH World's Champion" accompanying a large photo of Gotch dressed in sartorial splendor. That paper was usually published on Thursdays.

The *Tribune* story reported that Hackenschmidt tried three times in the last half hour of the contest to get the bout ended and a draw as the decision, but Gotch laughed at the notion, the crowd hooted and referee Ed Smith said, "Proceed with the bout. I am here to stay all night if necessary."

Then came the end.

"Hack approached Referee Ed Smith and said, 'I surrender the championship of the world to Mr. Gotch,'" Siler's story reported. Hackenschmidt went to his dressing room and declined any further action that night, the story added.

Wrestling as present Iowans know it for high school students was eight years from its first tournament when Gotch retired as world champion in 1913. According to school records, Iowa was in its third season of competition when Gotch hung up his boots. (Chapman used to own a pair of Gotch's wrestling shoes, which are now on display at the National Wrestling Hall of Fame's Dan Gable Museum in Waterloo.) Iowa State lists its first wrestling season in 1916, Cornell College in the 1922–23

Mike Chapman of Newton is the foremost authority on the history of Iowa-born world heavyweight champion Frank Gotch. Chapman, an author/historian and former journalist, is shown holding a Gotch poster while sitting in a chair that Gotch owned and wearing a hat Gotch owned. *Photo by Dan McCool.*

season and Northern Iowa (then known as Iowa State Teachers College) in 1923. All four schools won what has become known as the NCAA Division I wrestling team championship—an accomplishment unmatched by any other state going into the 2019–20 season.

The museum that was originated by Bev and Mike Chapman in Newton in 1998 reopened in Waterloo in 2007.

Coach Gotch? Governor Gotch? Chapman said an effort was made to have Gotch serve as head coach of the wrestling program at Iowa. E.G. Schroeder became the Hawkeyes' first coach and was a combined 5-2 in the first five seasons of the team. Gotch passed away in 1917, but Burns helped coach Cedar Rapids High School (now known as Cedar Rapids Washington) to the team championship in an invitational tournament at Ames in 1921. Five years later, the Iowa High School Athletic Association began sanctioning the event as an official state tournament.

Chapman said there was a movement started to have Gotch run for the state's highest office in 1920, but his 1917 death, at thirty-nine, closed that discussion. Decades later, there was a similar push to have Waterloo's Dan Gable enter the gubernatorial race, but he declined in 2001.

A longtime weightlifting enthusiast (he still pumps iron at seventy-five), Chapman said Gotch acquired much of his strength the honest way—doing farm work. That was the same for hundreds of state champions who grew up on farms and saw wrestling as an ideal activity because it took place in the winter. That meant it did not interfere with either the planting or the harvesting of corn and beans.

Chapman said the early team champions of Iowa high school wrestling such as Osage, Cresco and Fort Dodge had strong ties to farming. So did at least one future president.

"Wrestling, I've always maintained, has been a rural sport," Chapman said. "Abe Lincoln was a wrestler at New Salem, a tiny Illinois village, in 1832. There were about four hundred people living there. Jack Armstrong challenged him to a wrestling match. I've actually stood on the very spot twice where Abe Lincoln wrestled Jack Armstrong in 1832 and I've held seminars there."

Chapman grew up in a golden time for wrestling in Waterloo. The city's two public high schools, West and East, combined for eighteen team state championships—eleven for West, seven for East—between 1951 and 1977. In that same period, West was runner-up seven times and East twice.

His neighbors were the Buzzard brothers, Bob and Don Jr. They were both two-time state champions at East and all-America wrestlers at Iowa State. Bob was a member of the Greco-Roman squad for the 1972 Summer Olympics in Munich. Their father, Don Sr., was a state tournament finalist in 1934. He beat Harold Nichols in that state tournament. Nichols coached Bob and Don Jr. at Iowa State. The Buzzards would put a wrestling mat in their yard during the summer, and anyone missing a good wrestler could find him at the Buzzards' among the grapplers from Waterloo, Cedar Falls and anywhere else who wanted to keep their skills sharp.

"The Buzzards taught me how to wrestle by making me eat grass in their side yard every summer," Chapman said with a laugh. "They had their mat out, but a lot of times we ended up wrestling in the grass because there were so many kids there."

Chapman did not wrestle at East High, but he learned enough through his experiences with the Buzzards that he competed for a good navy squad during his three years of military service.

Jim Duschen, a fellow East High graduate and a longtime Chapman friend, described their hometown in the 1950s and '60s. "It was just a tough, blue-collar city. The work ethic that the people had was a large factor. Great coaches," Duschen said. "For one thing, it was the culture. They expected to win, they believed in what they were doing and didn't think anyone was supposed to beat them."

Duschen remembered that a boy growing up in Waterloo then didn't have to look far if he wanted to emulate a top wrestler. Duschen had a role model in his uncle Jack Smith, who won a state championship at East in 1953. Smith later became a Hall of Fame coach at Sigourney. Duschen qualified for the state tournament once in high school, then went from walk-on to all-American at Iowa State. He won two National Open championships in Greco-Roman, competed in the 1973 World Championship and later became a Hall of Fame wrestling coach at Basic High School in Henderson, Nevada.

"During that time, we lived in more of a disciplined culture. You respected people in authority—teachers, coaches—and whatever they told you to do, you did. I think that had a lot to do with it," Duschen said. "I think also seeing the success that the programs had. I looked up to guys at East High like Bill Dotson, Virgil Carr, Bob Buzzard. At West High there was Tom and Don Huff, Frank Lane, Lowell Stewart, guys like that who were state champions there. I looked up to those guys.

"Wrestlers were highly respected during that era, so a lot of youngsters coming up, they wanted to wrestle because they knew wrestlers were respected. There was a lot of interest and they were just tough, hard-nosed kids."

That described the people who shaped the state in the 1860s. Iowa achieved statehood in 1846, but roughly fifteen years later, the land was 50 percent forest. The land was considered fertile, but the Mississippi River on the east side of the state and the Missouri River on the west side were like ominous sentries protecting that ground.

Chapman said Gotch was a throwback to the people who turned soil in the place the Native Americans called "the beautiful land" as well as a role model for those who wanted to excel in a sport that lacks on-field support like football or on-court support like basketball.

"If there hadn't been a Gotch, I firmly believe Iowa wouldn't be wrestling-crazy," Chapman said. "I gave a speech in Missouri once and [someone said], 'You say it's the hard-core people who crossed the Mississippi.' Look how much guts it took to cross the Mississippi in the 1860s. You see this massive river, you've got all your family and their goods in this covered wagon behind you, your wife is saying, 'What are we doing?' and you build little rafts, you take that covered wagon and your animals and your family to the other side and then you forge into Iowa, which at that time was 50 percent forest.

"You come in here and you get hit by the winters, the Indians that don't want you here, you have to break the soil, cut down the forests, get a plow to break up the roots," Chapman continued. "Those are tough, tough, hardy people and there's your ingredients for great wrestlers."

The Mississippi River coursed through Minnesota and Missouri, as well as Iowa. The people in those two states seemingly had to be of the same double-tough spirit, but Chapman identified Iowa's difference. "Frank Gotch was the difference. We had Frank Gotch," Chapman said.

Chapman was serving as sports editor of the *Cedar Rapids Gazette* when he created a multi-chapter feature regarding wrestling in Iowa titled "From Gotch to Gable." It wound up being a life-changing work, not to mention the No. 1 sports series that year by the Associated Press. Chapman said he got a call from University of Iowa Press, which thought the series would make an excellent book.

"The spirit of Frank Gotch and what he meant to this state has lingered all these years, but it had completely faded," Chapman said. "I think the turning point was when I was sports editor of the *Cedar Rapids Gazette* and wrote a series called 'From Gotch to Gable' and the University of Iowa Press called me up and offered me an opportunity to write a book. And I made some extra money, so all of a sudden I found a new outlet. I could make money *and* I could do something great for wrestling."

Chapman learned while doing the book that Gotch was heavy on the mind of wrestling's top coaches in Iowa. Chapman spoke about Gotch and Burns with Dave McCuskey, who led ISTC to the 1950 NCAA championship before moving to a long career at University of Iowa.

"He just sat up and said, 'Those were my heroes. Everybody knew who Frank Gotch was,'" Chapman said of McCuskey's response. "Then I'm talking to Paul Scott for the book. Great coach at Cornell College, took them to the NCAA title in 1947. I'm leading him along and I said, 'Were you a fan of Frank Gotch?' [Scott replied], 'Oh my, say, yes. Every farm boy growing up in Iowa loved Frank Gotch.' Then I talked to Harold Nichols, who took Iowa State to many titles. 'Were you aware of Frank Gotch?' [Nichols replied], 'You couldn't live in Iowa and not be aware of Frank Gotch.' So you look at the three coaches who took colleges to their first national titles, they all basically said to me Frank Gotch was their hero."

Community pride was yet to be rivalled by other sports such as baseball or football in the late nineteenth and early twentieth centuries. The best solution was a wrestling match to find the toughest SOB. Lincoln thrived on such challenges, and Gotch learned that both from Burns and from his own encounters in all-comers matches. In 1899, at Luverne, Iowa, Gotch lost a two-hour match against a much older and far more seasoned Dan McLeod, who had taken the heavyweight title from Burns. The legend of that match listed McLeod hiding his identity under the disguise of being a furniture dealer. McLeod is alleged to have told Burns about the promising twenty-two-year-old Gotch.

After some matches in the Yukon and after winning and losing the American heavyweight championship, Gotch began to make his move toward the bout against Hackenschmidt and the Humboldt man's place in history. People reported Gotch being a genial man on the street, an easy mark for any fundraiser in Humboldt, but that changed when he changed into his work clothes.

"Gotch had a mean streak. He was like Jack Dempsey," Chapman said. "Everybody said Dempsey was the nicest guy you'd ever want to meet outside of the ring. Friendly and affable and everything, but the minute the bell went *ding*, something went ding in Dempsey. He turned into a killer. The minute the bell sounded for Gotch, he was all business.

"He had that allegiance to his state and to his community," Chapman added, "and that really endeared him to me. If he would have been a jerk, I wouldn't have written anything about him. I write stuff about people who I like and respect and who I want people to know about."

Duschen said he worked for a time after graduating high school and before he went to Iowa State. He was asked what his career would have been had he not experienced the quality mindset of Waterloo.

"If we wouldn't have had that environment we had during that time in Waterloo, I probably would have wound up….Well, I was working for the railroad. I may have continued there, I may have wound up in a plant like John Deere Tractor Works and had a regular blue-collar job," Duschen said. "I think of all of the experiences I've had in the sport, all of the people I've met, all the places I've been able to go. I represented the U.S. team in (Greco-Roman) in the World Championships in Tehran, Iran. Those were opportunities I would have never had if I had just stayed in Waterloo and worked."

The "what-if" question regarding Gotch gave Chapman a way to answer the question of a Texas-based reporter who happened through Iowa and stopped to witness a wrestling meet. The reporter was stunned by the crowd, estimated to be twelve thousand, and the unmistakable electricity. He was given Chapman's telephone number.

"I told him, 'Frank Gotch was Babe Ruth. If Babe Ruth would have been born in Humboldt, Iowa, we'd probably be a baseball-crazy state,'" Chapman said. "I think Frank Gotch really paved the way. Then Harold Nichols admired him, and he admired Farmer Burns. These were big-time heroes. They were like Tom Brady or LeBron James today, and they were from right here in the state."

Nichols was one of the game-changers in the sport of collegiate wrestling, Chapman said. There have been four distinct eras of the sport: the Ed Gallagher Era, the Harold Nichols Era, the Dan Gable Era and the Cael Sanderson Era. "Now there have been a lot of other great coaches: Port Robertson, Tommy Evans, Dave McCuskey, J Robinson, John Smith, Tom Brands, but those four coaches, in my estimation, changed the complexion of wrestling," Chapman said.

"Gallagher (Oklahoma State) was slick, take them down (he had a degree in engineering), he was an engineer, control, don't worry about pinning them. Nichols was take them down, beat the crap out of them and turn them. Larry Hayes of Des Moines Lincoln and Tom Peckham of Cresco were his first great stars, and very physical wrestlers," Chapman said. "Then along comes Dan Gable, who was just a perfect fit. Harold Nichols changed the concept of college wrestling. I used to go to the old (Iowa State) Armory and see crowds of four to five thousand back then, which was amazing. Gable took that Harold Nichols philosophy to Iowa, let's beat them up and turn them. He had the Banachs, Randy Lewis, Barry Davis, Jim Zalesky and people who bought into that style. And then Cael created his own style at Penn State."

Chapman believes Dan Hodge (an Oklahoma high school state champion, an undefeated wrestler at University of Oklahoma and an Olympic silver medalist in 1956) and Peckham (a three-time state champion at Cresco, a two-time NCAA champion at Iowa State and a member of the U.S. freestyle team at the 1968 Olympics) were modern-day versions of Gotch. But even they would not stand up to the man, Chapman said.

Make a match with no time limit, no points scored and the only way to win by pin or submission, and Chapman takes Gotch against anyone. Gotch had no obvious chip on his shoulder; he was just a one-in-a-million, naturally tough human being with natural wrestling instincts and ability according to Chapman.

"It's my estimation that the greatest wrestler who ever lived in those terms is Frank Gotch," Chapman said. "All the years I've been around the sport of wrestling, tough guys like Lou Banach (of Iowa)—who I think is the greatest college heavyweight ever—or Carlton Haselrig (of Pitt-Johnstown), who is right there; Kyle Snyder…anybody you want to mention, I think Gotch would have beat them under those rules."

Gotch passed away on December 16, 1917, from kidney failure, and the businesses and school in Humboldt closed on the day of his funeral three days later. The service was held at the Congregational Church, with Reverend Alexander Bennett, a friend of Gotch's, as the officiant. Among the large crowd at the service were Burns, Gotch's manager Emil Klank and Iowa governor W.L. Harding.

"I have known Frank Gotch for ten or twelve years both as a champion and as a private citizen. He always was a gentleman, kind and considerate. He was a true friend of clean sports and no man has done more to promote wholesome athletics," Harding said in a statement.

Chapman often uses a quote from the 1880s author Thomas Carlyle and his book *On Heroes and Hero Worship*. "Whoever excels in what we prize, appears the hero in our eyes," Chapman recited. "Frank Gotch excelled in what I prize…and many other Iowa lads, as well."

Another great Iowa influence was Earl Caddock, who came along shortly after Gotch hung up his boots. Caddock was like Gotch in that he grew up on a farm. Caddock was born in South Dakota but moved to Iowa when he was fourteen years old. Caddock's home was near Anita in southwest Iowa. Chapman said Caddock had an eye on making the 1916 Olympics after winning national AAU championships in 1914 and 1915, but World War I ended his amateur plans.

Caddock had a 53-0 record as an amateur, Chapman said, and he continued the winning ways as a professional wrestler with 26 victories. On April 9, 1917, Caddock put his perfect mark on the line in Omaha against world champion Joe Stecher of Dodge, Nebraska. After a pitched battle of more than two hours, Caddock took Stecher's title.

Caddock became one of the nation's more popular athletes in 1919 and 1920, on par with Ruth, Dempsey and Thorpe. But duty called, and Caddock enlisted in the army to fight in the war. He had served in France and sustained lung damage from gas attacks, Chapman recalled. Upon his discharge, Caddock returned to his Iowa roots just as Gotch had. Caddock wrestled for three more years and then retired from wrestling to begin what would be a successful career in business in Walnut and in Omaha.

"Earl Caddock was a devoted husband, father, Christian and highly successful businessman, as well as patriot and champion athlete," said Chapman, whose body of thirty books includes biographies of Caddock and Gotch. "His story is both heroic and inspirational."

Caddock passed away in 1950. He was feted locally and nationally.

"Overnight Caddock, who had always been a hero in the eyes of his southwestern Iowa friends and neighbors, became the toast of the entire state," wrote *Des Moines Register* sports editor Sec Taylor, a friend of Caddock's. "Perhaps no other Iowa athlete, not even Frank Gotch, caught the fancy and the imagination of the public as did Caddock until the late Nile Kinnick, Iowa football player, came along. Each had much in common in that they had personality, character, were deeply religious and excelled in whatever they tried to do."

Nat Fleischer, the top boxing and wrestling writer of the first half of the twentieth century, eulogized Caddock in his book *Milo to Londos*.

"He was an inspiration to the youth of America. During his entire career, he exemplified the best in American sports traditions," Fleischer wrote. "And when the history of wrestling is written…I shall see that Earl Caddock's name goes up near the top for his wrestling ability, and on top as the man who has done most for the uplift of wrestling in this country."

2
IOWA'S OLYMPIC GOLD

Dan Gable finally had reason to laugh. A twenty-three-year-old man from Waterloo, Iowa, became a worldwide sensation on August 31, 1972, when he beat Rusl Ashurallev of the Soviet Union, 3–0, in the gold medal match at 149.5 pounds during the 1972 Summer Olympics in Munich, Germany.

Gable never lost in high school at Waterloo West and lost once at Iowa State. He was like Brazilian soccer star Pelé in being known by a mononym—Gable—before Madonna made it fashionable. The USSR vowed to find a wrestler who would beat Gable, who predicted gold one year after he won a gold medal in the World Championship at Sofia, Bulgaria.

Gable is the oldest living member of the five products of Iowa high schools who climbed amateur wrestling's highest peak. Allie Morrison of Marshalltown (1928), Glen Brand of Clarion (1948) and Bill Smith of Council Bluffs Jefferson (1952) have passed on. Tom Brands of Sheldon (1996) is the most recent Iowan to earn a gold medal. Among the American individuals who have combined for forty-nine Olympic gold medals in freestyle, Gable is fourth oldest.

Maury White of the *Des Moines Register* filed a report of Gable receiving his gold medal: "He bent as the large gold medallion was draped around his neck. And as he straightened Dan took it in one hand, kissed it soundly—and laughed aloud."

On a spring day forty-seven years later, Gable explained his major break from rank. "I'd been waiting to laugh for a long time," he said. "I mean my

A HISTORY OF WRESTLING IN IOWA

Frank Gotch rose from Humboldt, Iowa farm boy to become world heavyweight wrestling champion. His fame earned him an invitation to the White House and a spot on the cover of magazines such as this 1916 issue of *National Police Gazette*. *Courtesy of Mike Chapman.*

wife says...she never saw me smile—and my kids backed her up—until I stopped coaching. So, between being an athlete and being a coach, I needed some laughter. Obviously, right when I won that gold medal, I was capable of doing some laughing—for a second or two."

Gable, Wayne Wells and Ben Peterson, Gable's teammate at Iowa State, were gold medalists in 1972. John Peterson, Ben's brother, and Rick Sanders were silver medalists and Chris Taylor, another Iowa State wrestler, won a bronze medal. The Soviet Union won five of the ten contested freestyle gold medals and added four more in Greco-Roman.

"I think it was my makeup. The fun was just being successful for me," Gable said. "I remember winning a state championship in swimming, I remember winning a state championship in wrestling. I don't think I ever jumped for joy except for maybe...after winning the gold medal, we were all together as medalists, and I looked at them and I go 'Yeah.' There's a picture of that. It's on the Internet. It's like, 'Did I just do that?' and they all looked at me like, 'Did he just do that?' It was a defining moment."

So was Gable's on-the-mat performance. He did not surrender a point during the competition. Ivan Yarygin of the USSR had six pins on his way to a gold medal in 1972, but Gable's body of work became the *uber* accomplishment. The artist LeRoy Neiman created a work titled *Gable's Gold*. Bobby Douglas, who wrestled Gable and later coached against him, said what Gable did was comparable to throwing back-to-back no-hitters in the World Series.

Much has been written about the summer morning in 1966 when Bob Buzzard, a two-time state champion at Waterloo East High School and two-time NCAA all-American at Iowa State, delivered a thumping to Gable on Gable's basement workout mat. Gable had angry tears that day, vowing to never miss a day of training.

Another motivator was a day early in his career at Iowa State, when Gable tangled with Cyclone 123-pounder Gary Wallman, an eventual two-time all-American. It was soon after the varsity was brought into practice after the freshmen had a few weeks of in-room training to themselves.

"I don't know whether I won that practice or (Wallman) won it, but I think he won it because by that time I was pretty much used to winning almost every practice," Gable said. "When I left, I remember walking down the stairs and going into the steam room. My thoughts were totally on re-evaluation—'Now wait a minute, if I'm going to be good here, what just took place with me, I'm going to have to have a little more commitment than I'm having.'"

Gable was born in 1948, the same year Brand got his gold medal. Gable was nearly four years old when Smith got his gold. Growing up, Gable did not have anything called the Internet to look at old films of Olympic champions for motivation. He did have goals and targets that most people his age either could not or would not comprehend.

"In my sport, that is the highest level," Gable said. "In a perfect world, is the professional league higher than the Olympics? As far as getting paid, that depends. I would say 'Yeah,' but there is an aura about it. It is the one time, ever since the invention of television, that everybody can watch the best competitors in the world. I do think the media is what really helped bring to everybody that high level of greatness of what's out there.

"There's nothing like picking up a newspaper and seeing something across the top of the paper. I'm not going to ever get over that. I'm never going to stop reading the newspaper. I mean the *Des Moines Register* hammered me after I lost (to Larry Owings in the 1970 NCAA finals). I will never forget that. I mean I knew I lost, but I really didn't know it until I read the *Des Moines Register*."

The banner headline "TITLE TO CYCLONES—GABLE FAILS!" on the cover of the March 29, 1970 "Big Peach" sports section would be a rare instance where Gable and winning were not in the same story.

Carl Adams, Gable's teammate at Iowa State, said he remembered Gable shed tears all the way to Ames from the tournament site, Evanston, Illinois. Others predicted Gable had a workout once the team returned as a response for a lone loss in 182 matches.

"I went right to the wrestling room," Gable said. "We drove to Beyer Hall; I grabbed two guys and opened the room and wrestled for an hour."

Two years later, "GABLE'S DREAM TURNS TO GOLD" was the banner headline in the September 1, 1972 *Register*.

Keeping his word to continue daily training, Gable got back to winning Gable-like as he prepared for the 1971 worlds and he got the mental sharpness back. Gable would coach the 1984 Olympic freestyle team to seven gold medals—including Hawkeye wrestlers Randy Lewis and twins Ed and Lou Banach—and he recruited several world and Olympic wrestlers to Iowa City, but he said getting himself ready for gold is easier than doing the same for others.

"When I went to the worlds, even though I didn't go unscored upon, I had won enough after Owings in dominant fashion to be pretty damn sure I was going to win," Gable said. "I never really focused on whether I was going to win or not either. I just focused more on competing hard because that's what I didn't do in the Owings match. I either wasn't able to compete hard or I just didn't compete hard, and I think it was a combination of both, but as long as I could compete hard I was pretty much going to win. I don't know if I ever felt that way about an athlete at the world and Olympic level, knowing that they're going to win. Pretty sure they're going to win, but are they that much better that it's going to be automatic? I don't know. I also look at it like it's a little more difficult from that point of view too because it's somebody else."

Brands concurred, "I knew that I was focused, I knew that this was No. 1 in my life. God, country and wrestling and that's my life…anything more in that little circle is too crowded. That's what you try to find, people who are like-minded."

Gable said he remembers moments in life that serve as a motivator, including the Buzzard workout; the murder of his sister, Diane, in 1964; and losing to Owings.

"A lot of people take that with a grain of salt maybe," Gable said. "I'm not one of those guys. There's a lot of meaning in a lot of first-time things for me."

Gable called the first-time Olympic gold medal his coolest sports accomplishment because of how it shot his name recognition into the stratosphere. "In my sport, it's made a big difference," Gable said. "I think it's given me a lot of confidence in my life. I think it's given me a lot of security. I think it's given me a lot of the ability to use that label to be able to help the sport and it continues to be able to do that. Obviously, it's very meaningful.

"If you're a baseball player, a football player or a basketball player, it's not exactly the same," Gable asserted. "You could start and at least get a big name there, be known everywhere, but for wrestling the Olympics… you look at 1980, when we didn't get to go to Russia, you look at the effect it had on Lee Kemp and then you understand it is the Olympics for wrestling. Yeah, we have world championships, but it is the Olympic year that can define somebody forever in wrestling."

Kemp, one of a select few American wrestlers to beat Gable, was a two-time world champion prior to the 1980 boycott ordered by President Jimmy Carter. Kemp won a then unprecedented third world title in 1982. Kemp was the youngest American world champion in wrestling—he was twenty-one years, eight months old in 1978—until Henry Cejudo was twenty-one years, six months old in winning Olympic gold in 2008. Kyle Snyder was nineteen years old when he won a gold medal in the 2015 World Championship.

Gable casts a different vote in regard to his accomplishments.

"I think my coolest moment probably was in Sofia, Bulgaria, winning the worlds the year before," Gable said, "just because I went from one platform to another, went from college wrestling to Olympic wrestling at the world level. Not too many people go into that jump and the very first time they win it. It was in an outdoor setting, 10,000 Bulgarians. It was at the end of a soccer stadium with tarps in case it rains—which it did. First time (my) parents weren't in the audience, they didn't make the trip. And it showed kind of who I was and where I was going, I think, even though we had Russian duals, went to Tblisi, won that. That actually put me in the category to be able to get all of the ink that was on me, that kind of made me stand out."

Some articles listed Gable among the gold medal favorites in 1971. It was twenty-two years later that Gable watched two of his athletes, Tom and Terry Brands, win gold medals in their first World Championship appearance in Toronto.

"That even means more; they weren't even favored to win it," Gable said.

Tom Brands is still amazed at the power of an Olympic gold medal, considering his twin brother's gold medals from the 1993 and the 1995 World championships.

"Terry's international career is more decorated than mine, and I get more fanfare because I won the Olympic Games," Tom said. "He's a two-time world champion and Olympic bronze (in 2000)."

Terry was beaten by eventual Olympic gold medalist Kendall Cross in the final Olympic Trials in 1996. Even though his dream was crushed, Terry provided his brother with an invaluable resource—mimicking the wrestling style of South Korea's Jang Jae-Sung, whom Tom beat in the gold medal match at Atlanta. Tom beat three former or eventual world champions—Abbas Haji Kenari of Iran, Sergey Smal of Belarus and Magomed Azizov of Russia—to get to finals.

"I'm telling ya, especially the finals match because I had wrestled the other three guys before, but especially the finals match (Terry) gave me a feel that felt (as if) when that whistle blew I had already wrestled him. He was a young Korean, but I didn't know him. Terry had given me that report in the warmup, not verbal but he wrestled just like that. It was almost outside the world familiar, and that's because you had a good support group," Tom said. "That's what good coaching does, somebody who is not just there for you, but they put the extra thought or extra effort into getting you what you need. But more importantly what they think is most important. What was most important was to give me the feel of a Korean who I'd never wrestled."

The Brands twins started wrestling in Sheldon, Iowa, in fifth grade. They learned quickly of the ultimate prize in amateur wrestling and locked on to that.

"We were very curious, and I remember researching the highest level. It was the Olympic Games, so right away we knew the pinnacle of the sport was the Olympic Games," Tom said. "Even though we probably wouldn't have framed it that way or said it that way, we knew what the pinnacle of the sport was. We slowly found out about Dan Gable, not Iowa so much but it was Dan Gable the Olympic champion. That was in 1979 when we started, and 1980 was a boycott year. The first wrestling camp I went to was an AAU camp in Lincoln, Nebraska. Chris Campbell was the headliner. He was on the '80 team, he sat home from Moscow and I remember him talking to the group. I was in fifth grade and I felt his pain so to speak."

Another point that was burned into their minds was seeing the televised matches of brothers Dave and Mark Schultz at the 1984 Olympics while the Brandses were at a camp in Colorado. They heard about the three Hawkeye wrestlers who won gold and another, Barry Davis, who was a silver medalist. A farmer named Randy Feekes showed them some basic moves and suggested they practice. They listened. Ron Still suggested saying goals into a mirror or writing them down on paper, sometimes doing it ten times. They did.

"I think a curious nature and a vivid imagination is rare, and the older I get the rarer it is. We had that. We had very vivid imaginations. I don't think it's very common," Tom said.

They kept an Olympic championship in mind as they grew in the sport, even if a classmate scoffed at Tom's saying what he would accomplish. They won a combined three state championships and a total of five NCAA championships. Their aggressive, attacking style broke opponents and turned some fans off, but they stayed focused. In a 1996 interview, Tom explained the burning desire to win: "I come from a family of fiery people who don't accept mediocrity."

"I guess as you got older, you don't apologize for success and how you get there," Tom said. "Everybody's not going to love you, and who really cares? We have to be gentlemen to a certain extent, but you're not going to have everybody's approval. Impossible to please everybody."

Tom described the workouts with Terry as two kids trying to be the alpha male and refusing to take a back step to the other.

They signed to wrestle for Gable at Iowa, beginning what Tom said was an excellent mentoring program. "Like having workout partners that held you accountable and that would beat the holy living tar out of you, but then at the end of that workout they would spend 45 minutes with you teaching you how to beat them, which was a great mentorship in coaching. Joe Melchiore, Randy Lewis, Brad Penrith, Barry Davis," Tom said. "Nobody was going to outwork our mentality. They were more skilled, they were better, they were talented, but you come to find talent can be defined a lot of different ways. Work ethic is talent, healthy stubbornness is talent, hunger is talent. Proving people wrong is a talent, it might be a little dysfunctional."

Toronto in 1993 was the first appearance on the world stage for the Brandses. The mindset was not new. "Nothing really changed because Toronto was the next tournament, so that's the one you focused on. You win that, you did your job."

Tom had two years of doubt built up by the time the Summer Olympics came to Atlanta in 1996. He did not do his job in Istanbul, Turkey, in 1994 or in Atlanta for the World Championships in 1995. (Terry won his second world title then.) But as Gable mentioned earlier, Brands did a lot of winning in a lot of places.

"The thing is I had competed a lot of places, I'd beaten all the favorites. The only guy I didn't beat was Sergey Smal, and I had him second round (in 1996). I had a world champ the first three matches. The Iranian won the world in '97, Sergey Smal was a world champ and silver in Olympic and Azizov was a world champ," Tom said. "I'd won Krasnoyarsk....I don't remember the doubters as much. I remember always having doubt as I remember it was a war politically against Sunkist Kids, Art Martori and his group. It was a war. It was Iowa against the world, and it really was in my mind. Whether I was delusional and making that up to give me a little extra kick in the pants or whether that was real...in my mind it was real. The people running USA Wrestling were the same people who were active politically against Alger and Terry and me. I'll tell you what, you've got two choices and you know what choices they are: put your head in the sand and quit or you can frickin' fight."

All to get to where he wanted to be when he was a boy.

"I remember my last meal was a bowl of cereal and banana. I remember being a little bit like maybe amped up and hyped. I just went to my routine," Tom said. "I like to read. I was reading a Louis L'Amour novel; I read and then I got drowsy, took a nap for 45 minutes, then it was time to get up and drink water or whatever your drink was, then get to the arena and get a warmup."

As the final seconds ticked off the scoreboard at the Georgia World Congress Center, future Cornell College coach Mike Duroe had a joyously long shout of "Tommyyyyy." Tom gave himself a verbal pat on the back in his post-match press conference: "I don't pat myself on the back very much. I'm pretty hard on myself when it comes to competition. When I feel good about myself, that's a rarity. I feel real good about my wrestling in the last couple of days."

Brands had given up one point en route to the gold—a takedown by Azizov late in their match—to add a modern exclamation point to what Gable accomplished twenty-four years earlier.

In 2019, Tom said the approach that day was the same.

"It was the next tournament on the calendar, it was the next match on the calendar. Go out and do your job," Tom said. "If you wrestle like you're capable of wrestling, nobody can beat you. That's been the philosophy from Day One. When it was over, you did your job. It was a pretty good tournament going through some pretty good competition."

One cool post-match item was the note Tom received from Terry. It closed with, "You did what we both know that we could do."

"That meant something to me because he didn't have a chance to do what we both knew we could do," Tom said, "but he gave me the ultimate credit."

Tom retired from competition after the 1996 Olympics. Terry went through one more quadrennium before hanging up his boots. Was that gold medal Tom's epitome?

"I think I'm still looking for that highlight," Tom said. "I think that my individual competition, my own competitive career, I think when you look back on it there was a track of things that were really, really positive. I don't give myself enough credit for sure. When you combine Terry's results with that, if you really stop and look at it, it's pretty impressive."

Tom even answered his own question when reflecting back on 1996.

"How can there be so much emotion in something trivial like a wrestling match? You dedicate your life to something, that's why," Tom said.

What gets Tom now is thinking of the epitaph most of a life in wrestling will afford him at the end, including the mention of being an Olympic gold medalist.

"It will say that and being from Iowa and having Iowa roots. I-O-W-A, four letters, that's probably the biggest thing," Tom said. "You look at Gable. Waterloo, Iowa, Bob Siddens, Iowa State, Harold Nichols, Iowa, Gary Kurdelmeier hired me and then I became Dan Gable Iowa. I mean look at that. For me, look at my lineage. My lineage goes back through Iowa State, Harold Nichols. And where did Harold Nichols go to school? Cresco. We're all linked pretty doggone close."

3
UNIVERSITY OF IOWA

Dan Gable and Bob Siddens were the epitome of the coach-athlete relationship ever since the 1962–63 season, when Gable was a freshman ninety-five-pounder in the Waterloo West High School practice room Siddens ruled with a golden hand.

Gable was christened Danny Mack Gable, but he was always "Daniel" when Siddens spoke of the redheaded kid who grew to be an undefeated, three-time state champion for the Wahawks. Siddens was always "Coach Siddens" when Gable spoke of the quiet man who led West to eleven state championships.

During one glorious stretch of his coaching career, Gable led Iowa to nine consecutive NCAA team championships. The run has a start and a finish in College Park, Maryland. It started in 1978 and ended in 1987, when Jim Gibbons led Iowa State—Gable's alma mater—to the team championship. That run remains unmatched going into the 2019–20 season. However, Nick Mitchell, head coach of NAIA member Grand View University in Des Moines, is seeking a ninth straight title in 2020.

In NCAA Division I, Penn State has an active mark of four consecutive team championships. Penn State is coached by another Iowa State graduate, Cael Sanderson, who was an undefeated, four-time NCAA champion.

"What's funny to me is because everybody's on the same level playing field in (NAIA), I don't know why somebody hasn't stepped up (to challenge Grand View)," Gable said. "He must be doing a good job to have that many competitive guys and, because of that, you have to commend him a lot.

Bob Siddens was Dan Gable's wrestling coach at Waterloo West High School. They are shown together at a wrestling gathering in Waverly. As coaches, Siddens and Gable had one thing in common: Their first team championship (Siddens in 1951 at West, Gable in 1978 at Iowa) did not have an individual champion. *Photo by Dan McCool.*

Because it takes even more people to become very good and he has that compared to everybody else, so that's amazing to me."

The domination has a familiar ring for at least one Hawkeye who was part of the original run of nine.

"Nick Mitchell at that level is Gable. He's gotten after it," said Ed Banach, a three-time NCAA champion under Gable at Iowa and a gold medalist in freestyle wrestling for the 1984 Summer Olympics team Gable coached. "Yeah, it's not Division I. Yeah, the finalists in the weight classes, they would have a hard time being in the top eight at the NCAA (Division I) tournament, but competitiveness is still competitiveness, and everything the same, he's doing a great job."

Gable's 15 NCAA titles are the most by any Division I wrestling coach, and he added 21 Big Ten Conference tournament titles in a career that started in 1976 and wrapped in 1997. He also led Iowa to a 355-21-5 record (a 94 percent success rate) in dual meets. Was the nine in a row a personal highlight of his career? Gable said it does not define him as a coach.

"I love the stat because it's a leading stat, but that's the only thing I love about it," Gable said.

When it came time to write a key chapter of their coaching careers, Siddens and Gable had a similarity: The first championship Siddens helmed at West in 1951 did not have an individual state champion. West had three wrestlers in the finals and wound up with four runners up and a third-place finish because of the wrestle-back rule to determine a true second place individually. The 1978 NCAA Division I championship for Iowa, which started the record run of gold trophies, had two finalists but no national champions. It was also remembered for 190-pounder Frank Santana of Iowa State sustaining a knee injury and having to default out of the championship match against Ron Jeidy of Wisconsin. Iowa State coach Harold Nichols called the match off, denying Santana a second straight NCAA title and giving the Hawkeyes a half point margin of victory over the Cyclones. It remains the narrowest victory margin in Division I tournament history.

The margin of victory in 1978 was far from the ordinary during Iowa's nine straight championships. The Hawkeyes averaged a margin of 34 points between themselves and second place during those years. Iowa set the scoring record four times during its run, reaching 158 points in 1986. That was over 73 points ahead of University of Oklahoma. The record stood until 1997, when Iowa scored 170 points in what would be Gable's final tournament as head coach in Cedar Falls, next door to his native Waterloo.

"I think it is (impressive), considering I've won by only half a point," Gable said. "When you look at it that way, it is, but if you look at how many points one guy can score, then it's not so dominating."

Much has been written about the Midas touch Siddens and Gable had in developing champion athletes and championship teams. Gable led University of Iowa to fifteen NCAA championships during his twenty-one-year coaching career. Siddens coached one season at Eagle Grove, where Tom Chelesvig was his first individual state champion in 1950, and then took over at West, where the eleven titles came in a twenty-seven-year effort.

Siddens was ninety-three when he passed away in 2018.

Siddens coined a popular description about coaching that can bring an instant smile to Gable or anyone else who heard it: "Coaching is a snow job. But it's a sincere snow job."

Gable talked about putting the sport in front of football crowds in Iowa City. The football team drew 70,000 fans to Kinnick Stadium, which is named for Nile Kinnick, Iowa's Heisman Trophy winner in 1939. Gable said he imagined a wrestling mat on the 50-yard-line on those Saturdays. Gable was retired when Iowa set the NCAA attendance record for a wrestling meet on November 14, 2015, drawing an announced crowd of 42,287 to Kinnick for an 18–16 victory over Oklahoma State.

Iowa broke its own scoring record at the NCAA tournament in 1981, then set it three more times during the nonuple. The 1986 mark of 158 points stood until 1997 (Gable's final NCAA tournament as head coach), when Iowa tallied 170 points, which remains the record.

"Great things happen sometimes just because of good planning," Gable said. "You're constantly looking for new things to be able to perform better, and that's why you have record performances along the line."

Gable spoke of perfection. He craved an NCAA tournament when ten Iowa wrestlers won first place. He coached the United States freestyle team in the 1984 Olympics at Los Angeles. During a spring speaking tour, Gable told a crowded room not to be too surprised if the team came home with ten gold medals. The powerful Soviet Union team did not compete in 1984, retaliating for the Americans' politically charged boycott of the 1980 Olympics. Team USA won seven freestyle golds, three by Iowa NCAA champions Randy Lewis, Ed Banach and Lou Banach. Another Iowa wrestler, Barry Davis, won a silver medal.

Was Gable crazy to think big about winning in such fashion?

"First of all, Gable's goal was to have ten national champions in one year. That was his goal and he was legit about it. Other people can say it, but they don't believe it. Gable really believed he could produce ten national champions," said Pete Bush, one of fourteen individuals to win a national title during the run of nine. "I'm sure Bill Gates is the same way, and anybody who is hugely successful, and that's Gable. I believed that we should have ten national champs at Iowa. You looked to the right and left of you, and they were all working out. You either do that or go home."

Bush said Gable became a father figure to him. Bush said his son, Daniel, is named for Gable and is better known as Danny Bush. The Bush family enjoyed a special moment in 2014, when Pete coached Danny to a Class 2-A state championship at Assumption.

Ed Banach added, "That was probably an unattainable goal, but he never took his sights off that because he knew in the process of going towards that, he would get five, six champions. I think the most he had one year was five? Is that right? When you shoot for the stars, you're going to land on the moon maybe."

Under Gable, Iowa had five NCAA wrestling champions in a single tournament twice: in 1986 (Brad Penrith, Kevin Dresser, Jim Heffernan,

Marty Kistler and Duane Goldman) and in 1997 (Jessie Whitmer, Mark Ironside, Lincoln McIlravy, Joe Williams and Lee Fullhart). Only Oklahoma State (1929, 1930 and 2005) and Penn State (2017) have joined Iowa in celebrating five champions in a season.

What Gable needed was ten people to survive the daily intensity that was practice at Iowa. Wait, he needed fifteen people.

"Dan Gable was the head coach, that name alone brought people to the state of Iowa, to the University of Iowa, to train with us. Before the world or Olympic trails would come up, these guys were in the room trying to make a world team," Barry Davis, a three-time champion, said. "People would come from all over to train in that facility, just to get ready to go for the world trials to make the team. People would come to Iowa and they'd go, 'What's the secret? What's the secret?' We'd go, 'What?' and they'd go, 'Tell us the secret. What's the secret in Iowa. Why are you guys so successful?' I'd go, 'There's no secret...' and three days later they'd be gone. They couldn't handle the day-to-day intensity that we trained with in the room."

Practice was scheduled for 3:30 or 4:00 p.m. most days. Preparation started earlier those days.

"You had to start thinking about workouts at 9:00 in the morning for a 4:00 workout. If you weren't ready, it would be a tough day in the room," Davis said. "Your mind was at a different level; your brain went to a different level because it had to be. The training every day was so difficult, it was just so hard. Your body and your mind just got used to that type of training. That type of intensity was just normal. A lot of guys were like, 'I'm out of here, I can't handle this, it's too crazy.'

"Their training partners were different than our training partners," Davis said. "In our facility, you had an Olympian, a national champion or an all-American to work out with every day. Or a former national champion or Olympian. I had Dan Glenn, Keith Mourlam, Randy Lewis, Kevin Dresser, Greg Randall...those were my training partners."

Ed Banach said having a lineup ready for a meet or a tournament included having some reserves being as battle-ready as the regulars. Hence, there were fifteen guys ready to go.

"That was the beauty about Gable. The way you worked it was you had ten weight classes, so you better have fifteen people ready. Those five in waiting are backups for every two weight classes," Ed said. "Every two weight classes had a third man that if somebody got hurt and couldn't go, you were expected to cut down or you were expected to step into the weight class. Gable made sure, Robinson made sure, Yagla made sure,

Johnson made sure they knew who the fifteen guys were and they worked with them."

Today, Sanderson and Penn State are the talk of college wrestling, just as Gable and Iowa were in the 1980s and the 1990s. Gable said there could be similar paths to success.

"Cael's not just winning because he's winning," Gable said. "He's doing some things that's obviously (better) and he's developing kids into better wrestlers. Maybe it's easier to recruit because people want to go there, maybe have more numbers, but it's still what you're doing with those kids and who's leading that group as a coach, as a staff, as a leader in the room as an athlete.

"My best teams…not only were the coaches doing well," Gable said. "I didn't have just Barry Davis in there; I had Barry Davis, I had Ed Banach, I had Lou Banach, right up the line. When I had the two Brandses, I had the two Steiners, I had all those names. It wasn't just one. It might have started with one, but all of a sudden you had seven or eight that were affecting the total team. Then it wasn't just the ten guys, it was the twenty-five guys or thirty-five guys. That thirty-fifth kid was competitive."

Gable's legend as a competitor was fueled by his only loss in high school or college—a 13–11 defeat as a senior at Iowa State by Larry Owings of University of Washington in the 1970 NCAA tournament finals. Gable won a world championship in 1971 and then became *Gable* in the 1972 Summer Olympics by not surrendering a single point on his path to the gold medal.

His coaching legend started when Iowa hired Gable from intrastate rival Iowa State to be Coach Gary Kurdelmeier's assistant and eventual replacement. Gable became head coach for the 1976–77 season and had the Hawkeyes on top of the wrestling heap one season later. They stayed there until his alma mater budged in front at the 1987 tournament. Between the start of the streak in 1978 and the end in 1987, Iowa was 174-8-1 in duals and *averaged* seven and a half all-Americans per season. Fourteen wrestlers tallied a total of twenty-three national championships.

"He was a great wrestler, but he was a better coach because he understood that not every wrestler is going to be able to do the same things he did, but he was going to challenge them saying, 'Hey, you came here, you wanted to become a champion, what are you going to do to become a champion? I'll tell you if you're on the right track or not,'" Ed Banach said. "He also understood that he had weak spots, and where his weak spots were, he hired coaches: J Robinson, Chuck Yagla, Mark Johnson…those guys filled in the gaps that Gable had."

Bush wanted to be a part of something great. It was in his blood. Bush's father, John, played football at Notre Dame and was a member of the 1949 undefeated national championship squad. John Bush was also heavyweight champion of the legendary "Bengal Bouts" intramural boxing program at Notre Dame. In 1979, Pete was the first individual to win a state wrestling championship at Davenport's Assumption High School and then won a Junior Nationals freestyle championship.

"I look back, and you have a different mindset when you're a younger kid, but today I'm thinking why the hell I would have ever gone to Iowa when the Banachs were just recruited ahead of me the year earlier?" Bush said. "You go in there, and I remember very vividly just having no doubt about my abilities. I will say Gable was never big on compliments, but the fact that they recruited me meant I was something. They liked what they saw, between he and J Robinson, and that was enough for me.

"I don't know for the life of me why I even went there, honestly, other than Gable was the coach and J Robinson was the assistant and they were, in my opinion, equally as effective for me. I'm watching the Big Ten championship as a senior in high school at Iowa City and obviously thinking that team is all-world, which it was, and all of these people—Bruce Kinseth specifically—just watching him wrestle and I just wanted to be part of that."

Kinseth was worth watching. On his way to an NCAA championship in 1979, Kinseth pinned each of his last nine opponents—four in the Big Ten tournament, five in the NCAA meet—and walked away with the outstanding wrestler award and the Gorriaran award for most pins in the NCAA tourney.

The wrestlers who wore Iowa's black and gold singlet were big on being goal-minded before they had Gable and company in their ears and in their path. Tradition helped ramp up the volume of seeking success.

"When you put on that singlet, you put on tradition. You put on past national champions, past national championships—a standard to uphold," Davis said. "You're part of the elite of the elite, and you're expected to do a certain thing—win, and that's it. You didn't want to let Dan Gable down. You didn't want to lose and walk back and look at him eye to eye. You knew what he was about, what he put in the program."

Bush added, "Just having him telling me what to do…I mean I really, really, really thought I was a hard worker in high school until I went to Iowa, and it was like my definition completely changed the first day…the first week if not the first day."

Ed and Lou Banach came to Iowa City from Port Jervis, New York. Ed was five minutes older than Lou. When he was twelve years old, Ed watched the 1972 Olympics on television. That was Gable's gold, and it became the launching pad of Ed's goal. Gable was at Iowa, and a few years later so was Ed.

"My goal was to be an Olympic champion, and I knew I had to surround myself with people who had similar, if not the same, goals," Ed Banach said. "Steel sharpens steel, so one man sharpens another, so that action is what I settled on. Gable wanted to win national championships. Gable wanted his athletes to win Olympic gold medals and it was that simple."

There were some uber-talented individuals on Gable's teams, particularly during the long streak, but Gable got into the Siddens coaching handbook by not trying to craft every Hawkeye in his design.

"What he did was just allow you to be what God wanted you to be as a wrestler," Bush said. "Gable understood there's plenty of ways to skin a cat and allowed you to wrestle the way, in my opinion, God intended you to wrestle. They didn't change anything. They just made what I came into college and made it better. I didn't wrestle anything like I did in high school at the end of my college career. Honestly, that's what Cael Sanderson's doing now."

Gable would do anything to give his wrestler an edge or, as a result of that edge, a victory. Ed Banach found that out after another frustrating loss to Iowa State's Mike Mann during the 1982–83 season.

"I lost to Mike Mann three times and beat him in the finals of nationals that year. After the January loss to Mike over here in Ames, I asked Gable, 'What do I got to do to win?' He said, 'You're going to have to start working out at 4:00,'" Ed recalled.

Ed remarked to Gable that he was already working at 4:00 p.m., often until 6:00 p.m. "(Gable) goes, 'That's not the 4:00 I'm talking about,'" he said.

Three days a week, Ed had 5:00 a.m. workouts at the Fieldhouse. "Gable was working on me mentally, and that was the year I tore my (ACL) in the Midlands, so I was going through rehab with that. Long story short, we watched the video of me wrestling Mann, he goes, 'Here's the weakness....' We worked on it every day from the middle of January to the middle of March. I would drill that technique over and over, so I didn't even have to think about it. If it presented itself, I just did it. In the finals of nationals that year, that's exactly what I did. I took off the Russian 2-on-1, hit the high crotch and took Mike down. Mike's left leg was hard to take down and he always kept it back, so I was able to get it out front and I was able to take him down with it."

Gable was still *Gable*, as in an autograph target for even the slightest fan. He signed everything from the brim of a hat to a Bible, even in the Bible Belt. Davis recalled a trip to Auburn, when Gable was trying to help keep the sport alive at that Southeastern Conference school, which hosted the 1971 NCAA tournament. Iowa won the meet, 42–0, and Auburn eventually dropped its program.

"We walked in the gym, and people just wanted to touch us," Davis said. "We just did our job, you know, and people were walking around like we were the '85 Chicago Bears you know? People going nuts over you."

Some may have thought Iowa's winning streak was in jeopardy during the 1983–84 season. Gable took a leave from his head coaching duties with the Hawkeyes to prepare for his time as head coach for the Olympic team. Robinson served as interim head coach and led Iowa to victory in fourteen consecutive duals, but a 24–6 whipping at Oklahoma State on February 10 brought Gable back to the college fold. The Hawkeyes answered questions by winning the conference tournament and then putting a nearly 26-point distance between them and second in the NCAA tournament. Iowa had five finalists, including Jim Zalesky, the outstanding wrestler of the tournament, who won his third championship and stretched his victory string to eighty-nine in a row.

Zalesky was one of four Iowa wrestlers to be voted outstanding wrestler of the NCAA meet during the nine-title run. The others were Davis, Kinseth and Marty Kistler. Zalesky and Davis were high school teammates at Cedar Rapids Prairie.

"I would say there's ten people, so there are ten different stories. I was a senior, and I was a captain. I had redshirted, but I was a national champ, so I was expected to do quite well. We won it even though I didn't even place—I won one match, then lost and didn't get a wrestle-back," Bush said. "The champion was Bill Scherr, who I pinned twice. The guy that got second I beat 18–3, Baumgartner, and the guy who got third I beat 11–2 in the Big Ten finals ten days earlier and I'm sitting on the sidelines. We had Greg Randall show up as a freshman; he was a national finalist that year, and you had people that were supposed to do well such as myself that didn't, and you had people that nobody thought would do well did. It's kind of like with the ten stories you have with the starting lineup and the belief in Dan Gable as the coach. Magic happens, end of story, and that's what happened to us."

One month after the 1984 championship, Robinson resigned over a dispute with University of Iowa administration regarding the intensive wrestling camp he and John Marks had created. Robinson was named head coach at Minnesota in 1986, and his 2000–2001 squad won the NCAA championship in Iowa City. Minnesota, in finishing 13 points ahead of the Hawkeyes, became the first team to have ten all-Americans.

If Gable and Robinson were together now, Bush said Sanderson would have fewer championships.

"I don't think there was any luck involved. If you're going to do that, be consistent like that, it comes down to leadership, which was Gable and Robinson. I just think if they were still together, it would still be going on regardless of Cael Sanderson showing up or not," Bush said. "I'm not sure why (Gable) retired. I'm still scratching my head why. They had a system, and it's a combination of the leadership and the kids, wrestlers, the athletes, whatever you want to call them, believing in the system and not questioning anything. You've got to go on blind faith sometimes."

Gable added, "I never thought of it that way, but enough people have told me and made me think about it a little bit. That's a very good possibility that the amazing run would have extended."

As the 1986–87 season dawned, Iowa had a new addition to its black singlet with gold trim and lettering: an X on the left thigh. That stands for ten in Roman numerals. The 1986 championship matched Iowa's wrestling team with the Yale golf program (1905–13) and USC's track and field teams (1935–43) for having won nine national titles in a row. The team's poster featured a ten-inch by ten-inch X.

"We're being a little cocky, I guess. I don't see it as cocky; I see it as motivation," Gable said at media day for the season. "If you don't look a little cocky in wrestling, you're not confident, so…"

Ed Banach said the X on the singlet might not have been Gable's idea, but he could make good use of it. "Gable always tried to motivate you. He motivated you in a lot of different ways. I think that was a way to motivate them. Turns out that it backfired a little bit, but it's OK," Ed said.

The Hawkeyes had reason to feel cocky. They had five returning all-Americans, including NCAA champions Brad Penrith and Jim Heffernan, leading the team.

As it turned out, none of the three programs won ten in a row.

Maybe Gable's media day comment about success crossing Iowa's eastern border was a harbinger of things to come. He said, "I've never lost to a team east of the Mississippi River," in talking about an early-season trip to Penn State. A 27–15 loss December 3, 1986, ended Gable's best-in-the-east string. Penn State was also the first visiting team to beat Iowa at Carver-Hawkeye

Arena, 19–18, on February 6, 1988—halting a stretch of forty-six successive wins on the home mat.

Iowa's other loss in the 1986–87 season was a 23–12 road defeat in the first of two meets against Iowa State. The Hawkeyes won, 18–15, in the return contest.

The NCAA streak ended where it started—in College Park, Maryland. The title-clinching pin by Bill Kelly at 126 pounds was shown live on *Wide World of Sports*. Ed Banach was there as an assistant to Iowa State's Jim Gibbons. Iowa State had a glimpse of the future when it beat Iowa in a dual meet. Banach, Les Anderson and Gibbons had plenty to celebrate, but there was no huge celebration that evening for what they now call "Cyclone Nation." Ed said some of the Iowa guys showed up and offered congratulations.

"There wasn't even a social planned," Ed said. "We just went to the oyster bar at College Park, Maryland, to have dinner and next thing you know a party broke out. The die-hards of wrestling came by and they showed respect. That was what was important. I was very happy for Iowa State and all the wrestlers that I'd coached. It's wonderful for them, I was so happy for them, but then thinking about what it meant to Gable….If anybody wins fifteen national championships for any team, that's pretty good."

One of the more overused words in sports is *dynasty*. Ed agreed two or three championships does not a dynasty make, but nine in a row epitomizes the definition.

"We're looking back and being nostalgic about it, but I've heard some people say those were the glory days. When I first got there, we set the example, we set the standard and they recruited to it," Ed said. "Basically, if you wanted to be the best you went to Iowa during that period and they went on and won. You still had to do the work, but you're putting yourself in the best atmosphere. It was almost mythical…they had it going. They had all the pieces to the puzzle."

What ended at nine could have grown to an even more outrageous number, Davis said. Iowa had a four-year drought of championships and then reeled off three in a row and then six between 1991 and 2000. Gable's final season was the 1996–97 campaign, which had the NCAA meet in the UNI-Dome at Cedar Falls (a few miles from where Gable grew up), and Iowa set the point record of 170 that still stands. He took a leave of absence for a season and then quietly slipped into retirement. Jim Zalesky was head coach for the last three titles in that string.

"There were little cracks in the armor, but he didn't really change things because he was still winning," Davis said. "It took him a while to get it back

Simon Roberts of Davenport became the first African American to win an Iowa high school state wrestling championship in 1954. Roberts became the first black NCAA wrestling champion in 1957, wrestling for University of Iowa. *Photo by Dan McCool.*

again, but when he got it back he won what, three or four more years in a row, I think. It took him a while to get back on track again; that's how far off track we were. If Gable would have taken care of business or made changes he should have made before that, there wouldn't have been a four-year gap. I think he would have won those four years and then the next four years again. That would be seventeen in a row. That's the way I look at it."

Gable said the success was such that he didn't catch the "little cracks in the armor" until 1987—the year Iowa State ended Iowa's run—"which is hard to believe."

"What that did for me was have me learn again and analyze again and, had I waited much longer and we still won, might have taken me longer to come back and win again," Gable said. "I think I was far enough gone that I needed that loss to help me win after that, even though I didn't understand why we weren't winning the next year and the next year and the next year until I analyzed later on. Once I analyzed later on, once you start winning again and you look at the whole program, then I could see it took a while to deteriorate and so it's going to take a while to build back up. I'm saying deteriorate means we went one step down, and that hurts."

Iowa returned to the top spot in the national tournament in 1991, and the Hawkeyes won nine of the next ten tournaments. Gable would later serve the program as an assistant coach when Tom Brands was hired to replace Zalesky in the 2006–7 season. Brands led Iowa to its most recent three championships in 2008, 2009 and 2010.

Davis said the "what if's" of comparing what Gable did to Duke coach Mike Kryczewski in basketball and Alabama coach Nick Saban in football would be off-the-charts expensive for colleges.

"If Coach K from Duke won the ACC twenty-two years in a row and he was in the Final Four every year but once out of twenty-two years, what do you think people would be saying about him? You couldn't pay him enough money," Davis said. "If Nick Saban won twenty-four SEC titles in a row and fifteen national championship and took second what, five times?"

Mitchell has an opportunity to match Gable's string at the NAIA meet, but will there be another Division I program that equals or exceeds what the Hawkeyes did for nine consecutive years? Bush hopes not.

"As proud as I am about the nine I was associated with, I hope that doesn't happen. Not because I don't want anybody else to do it, I just don't think it's good for the sport," Bush said. "I think that watching Penn State win year in and year out these days quite honestly is boring. I love the greatness and I love Cael Sanderson and his demeanor on the corner of the mat, but it takes the excitement out. I think as good as Cael Sanderson is, I don't think he'll go nine in a row. I think it's one of those perfect storm things that Gable created, he and J. Robinson. I'd be surprised if it ever got equaled or passed."

4
IOWA STATE

Harold Nichols denied University of Rhode Island becoming a hot spot of NCAA Division I wrestling as he turned a respected Iowa State program into one of the elite squads in the country.

Nichols, a farm boy from Cresco, Iowa, seemed to find success in everything he did. He did not win a state high school championship (his brother, Don, did it twice, while Harold's best finish was third) but earned an NCAA championship in 1939 while attending University of Michigan and wrestling for Coach Cliff Keen. He was a lieutenant in the army, earned a doctorate in education and won 529 college dual meets (492 of them in thirty-two years at Iowa State) and six NCAA team championships in thirty-seven years of coaching. He was known as "Nick."

There was a strong Iowa presence on his teams in Ames. The Cyclones had fourteen products of in-state high school programs win NCAA championships such as three-time winner Larry Hayes of Des Moines Lincoln and two-time winners Les Anderson of Clarion, Ron Gray of Eagle Grove, Tom Peckham of Cresco, Dan Gable of Waterloo West and Jason Smith of Ankeny. If the Cyclones were not winning the team title, they were almost a constant in the win-place-show of the trophy hunt. Iowa State had twenty-three top-three finishes during the Nichols era.

"I think the success of the team had a lot to do with it. He was I'd say ahead of his time as far as recruiting, getting excellent wrestlers," said Jim Duschen, a walk-on from Waterloo East who placed fifth in the 1969 NCAA tournament. "Nick could see that in the individuals. Larry Hayes,

A History of Wrestling in Iowa

When Kevin Dresser became Iowa State's wrestling coach in the 2017–18 season, he wanted to put the mat in places other than its regular home at Hilton Coliseum. This was a meet staged at nearby C.Y. Stephens Auditorium, giving it more of a setting of an opera house. *Photo by Dan McCool.*

for instance, was a one-time state champion out of Des Moines Lincoln. Pretty raw, but Coach Nichols could see the raw talent that he had, so he approached him and told him he'd like to have him wrestle at Iowa State. Larry had no idea what he was going to do."

What Nichols and assistant coach Les Anderson—Iowa State's first NCAA champion of the Nichols era—managed to do with recruiting on the eastern side of the United States and on Long Island, New York, in particular, kept Rhode Island from being more than just the smallest of the fifty states in area. The Cyclones landed future two-time NCAA champion Carl Adams and all-Americans Bob Antonacci and Pete Galea out of Brentwood High School on Long Island. Rhode Island coach Alan Nero wanted all three and a few others to wrestle where the state song is "Rhode Island, It's For Me."

"If (Nero) would have gotten all the guys he was trying to get, Rhode Island would have been national champions," Antonacci said. "He was trying to get Nick Gallo, who became a national champion. Me and Pete (Galea), all-Americans; Scott Pucino was an all-American, Willie and Charlie (Gadson) were all-Americans. We would have had a whole team of all-Americans if he was able to (pull it off), and he almost did because he's a really good salesperson."

Adams said there could have been big things in "Little Rhody."

"They had it going on. I think we would have had a good thing there because Alan Nero, who was a go-getter, he understood recruiting," Adams said. "He was an assistant coach there before he became head coach. He had been a former college wrestler, and he wanted to build that program at Rhode Island University because that's where he lived. He was headed in the right direction and did a great job, and then lo and behold the athletic director dropped it."

The difference between Rhode Island and Iowa State meant any success might not have lasted at the former, Adams said.

"I'll tell you exactly what would have happened. We would not have had the success we had at Iowa State. You're hearing that from a guy that wrestled at Iowa State. I actually coached six years at Iowa State, and I coached college wrestling for forty-one years. We would not have had the success that we had at Iowa State," Adams said. "Think about going into a room with Dan Gable, Ben Peterson, Chuck Jean, Jason Smith, Dave Martin, Jim Duschen and battling with those guys every day. You couldn't duplicate that situation in Rhode Island. The other thing to think about, when you were going to compete, it wasn't against University of Connecticut, U. Maine or Boston University. It was against Oklahoma State, Oklahoma University, Iowa, Lehigh....It was going to be against the best competition you could find in the country. All of that talent from a mental and physical standpoint, and if you're not used to going against that type of competition every day or on a weekly basis, you're going to have a heck of a time trying to get to that point we got to at Iowa State because it's all about building everything—strength, speed, confidence, knowledge—on a daily basis. You weren't going to get that at Rhode Island."

Antonacci said Nichols was not the greatest technical coach, but he provided an atmosphere where everyone could excel in Ames. You had the coaches and the workout partners. All you needed were your *cojones*. "For example, my weight class. I get in there on scholarship and there were four other guys on scholarship that were three- or four-time state champs. We had to battle out just to make the team," Antonacci said.

Nichols put a future two-time national champion and a combined six all-America honors in the room when Adams and his future roommate, Phil Parker, accepted scholarship offers. Adams said Iowa State began recruiting him after Anderson watched him work out at a training camp in the Great Lakes Naval Station in suburban Chicago for the Junior Olympics in August 1968.

"This is what I found out later on. Les said that when he saw me, I guess I really piqued his interest...and we had a chat," Adams said. "That's where Les saw me, and I guess Coach Nichols followed up on Les's recommendation. He flew me out to Ames on a recruiting trip. That's where I met my roommate-to-be, Phil Parker, on that recruiting trip. I also met Jason Smith and a few other guys who were already on the team. That ended up being my only recruiting trip, and part of it was because Coach Nichols reminded me so much of my high school coach (Joe Campo)—his demeanor and all of that. When he offered me a full scholarship, that's all I needed to hear. I didn't know much about the program or even Iowa State wrestling, I had heard they were pretty good. Gable's name wasn't quite as big as it ended up being. (Parker) and I decided that we would both go to Iowa State before I left Ames on that recruiting trip."

Antonacci said he and Galea wanted what Adams had. "Knowing that Carl was out there, and they were the No. 1 school, we had a good contact," Antonacci said. "We (talked to) Carl and said, 'How can we get out there?' He said, 'You're going to have to win the state championships a couple times at least because they only bring out state champions there.'"

Galea added, "I wanted to be like Carl Adams when it came to takedowns and things like that, but I never really could. I still tried to emulate him. I would even want to walk like he would walk, thinking that would help me get my takedowns or something."

Antonacci won a pair of New York titles, but Galea got upset on the way to getting to state. He made amends in freestyle by pinning the individual who won his weight at the state meet. The junior high rivals who became teammates and close friends in high school were a package deal, and Adams got Nichols and Anderson to look at them. When they came to Ames to wrestle, Antonacci said he frequently worked out with Anderson, a noted technician. Anderson came back to Iowa State in 1964 after coaching at Blue Earth High School in Minnesota. He left after the 1973–74 season to be head coach at University of Washington.

"He's the one who helped me grow the most in the wrestling room," Antonacci said. "When he left to go to Washington I was really, really upset because my last two years he was gone. I knew he would have helped me to excel."

Galea, a two-time all-American who was Iowa State's first four-time conference champion, said University of Rhode Island had his attention because of a good program in marine biology. Nick got the last word, which was often the case in recruiting battles.

"Nick explained to me that if you want to do marine biology, you've got to do biology probably first anyway," Galea said. "'We have a great biology program, so you're all set,' Nichols said. I took the biology at Iowa State, and…I got twelve credits in marine biology when I was at Iowa State. Nick really took care of people."

Antonacci said he'd rarely left Long Island before he and Galea boarded an airplane to make a recruiting visit to Iowa State.

"I didn't even know where Iowa was. I looked on the map and then went, 'OK, it was in the middle of the country, no big deal,'" Antonacci said. "Then when we went flying on the airplane, I looked down and I saw open land and I said to myself, 'Oh, Iowa's in the desert.' All we cared about was going to the best school in the nation, and they were the best school in the nation. They won two national championships just prior to when we got out, and when we got out there in 72–73, they won another championship. It was definitely the team of the decade. That was the place to go if you wanted to be the best."

Adams said Nichols had an early step ahead of a lot of his coaching brethren.

"Nick was ahead of his time in understanding the value of recruiting. For a number of years when I was there, after and probably even before, I think Nick understood recruiting probably better than any other coach in college wrestling at that time," Adams said. "You'd have to put Myron Roderick up there because he was a hell of a recruiter as well. Nick brought in the type of athletes that fit his mold of competitiveness. It was like if you got enough of them in that room, you couldn't help but have a great team. Nick found that channel for quality wrestlers and what he did was he stuck with it until the well ran dry. Nick was a brilliant man in his coaching style, the way that he got along with his athletes. His wrestlers wanted to work hard and win for him just because of the type of person he was. It came through loud and clear that he cared for his athletes. I give him a lot of credit for finding these quality recruits, bringing them to campus and getting them to sign. He was a very good businessman, and he was a great coach. He knew that if you rubbed steel on steel, if you put enough of them in the room, they were all going to get better real fast."

When Galea and Antonacci came to Ames on their recruiting trip, one part could have been disastrous. Anderson was giving them a tour of the campus, which included what was known as "Sorority Circle"—the large homes where numerous coeds resided. Anderson said this might be an area that interested the guys, but Galea said he spoke for Antonacci in that they were in no way going to join a sorority. Galea remembered Anderson's reply: "Well, I'm not sure they'd let you in."

What they lacked in knowledge of the Greek system, they made up in self-confidence. Antonacci noticed posters of guys promoting the season. He learned that earning all-America honors afforded a wrestler space on the display. He and Galea were ready to pose for the next poster in their polyester outfits—it was the disco era, Galea said. Nichols was not a man of flamboyance or excessive laughter. When he lowered his bifocal glasses down his nose and looked at you, something got his attention. Galea remembered seeing Nichols lower his glasses when Antonacci offered himself as a model.

There was no hesitancy in coming over 1,100 miles to wrestle, especially when Nichols offered both Galea and Antonacci a full-ride scholarship.

"I wasn't hesitant at all; I was pretty excited about it because I got a full scholarship. I was going to be able to finish school without having any debt, and I'm going to be wrestling with the best team in the country," Galea recalled. "There's not a lot to think about. And then when I got to Iowa, I met everybody, and I just really liked the people. Everybody was so nice."

Antonacci added, "When we got recruited, we didn't know what was going to happen because there were so many other recruits there too. Just because you came in for a recruiting trip doesn't mean you're going to get offered a scholarship. When Nick sat down and said, 'OK, this is what we're going to do,' it was like, 'OK, I just won the lottery.'"

There were others from the East Coast who came to Iowa State and were all-Americans, including the aforementioned Gadson brothers and Mike Picozzi. They were among thirty-one men who totaled fifty-seven all-America honors (including eleven national championships by eight men) between the 1970–71 and the 1979–80 seasons. Iowa State won three team championships during that span.

University of Rhode Island dropped its wrestling program at the end of the 1980–81 season. Carl Adams was the head coach. He would later serve as head coach at Boston University, which dropped its mat program at the end of the 2013–14 season. In 1981, Nichols led Iowa State to a third-place finish in the national tournament at Princeton, New Jersey. Jim Gibbons, who would take over as head coach when Nichols retired in 1985, and Nate Carr were national champions.

Nichols was hired at Iowa State after the Cyclones' Hugo Otopalik died in the summer of 1953. Otopalik and the Cyclones played host to the first NCAA tournament in 1928. Originally, he was hired as an assistant in Ames, then agreed to be interim head coach in 1923 when Charles Mayser resigned. The interim tag was dropped, and Otopalik held the job for twenty-nine years until his passing. One report had Nichols as the only candidate school officials interviewed for Iowa State's wrestling job. Nichols had been at Arkansas State since 1948 as head coach in track and field and swimming as well as an assistant in football and basketball. He started the wrestling program there in 1949.

The greatness of Iowa State's wrestling program is largely due to Nichols, according to former Iowa State coach Bobby Douglas. Nichols recruited Douglas—a two-time Ohio high school state champion—as an assistant coach, watched Douglas lead Arizona State to the 1988 NCAA team title at Hilton Coliseum in Ames and saw Douglas become Iowa State's fifth wrestling head coach in the 1992-93 season.

"If there was no Harold Nichols, there probably would have been no Dan Gable. If there wasn't a Harold Nichols, there probably wouldn't have been guys like Les Anderson, Chuck Jean, Ben Peterson," Douglas said. "Nick saw talent, he could see talent, and if you look back through the record books, he had recruited some of the best athletes in America. Not only that, he supported them. He made sure they got to the competition and he made sure they had good workout partners."

Galea concurred: "If I had gone to Rhode Island, I might have had some good opportunities too, but nothing like Iowa State. It was a magnet for great athletes. Joe Zuspann, Kelly Ward, Bobby Holland, Donnie Zimmerman… Iowa State was a magnet for great athletes, so one of the things that Iowa State did is it allowed me to be a part of a national championship team, which would never have happened with any of the other (schools). Without Nick running the show, Iowa State would not have been a national champion in my opinion. We all owe Nick a lot."

Douglas said he passed on wrestling at Iowa State because it was too far from his family, even though Nichols was the first big-time coach to recruit him. He was an NAIA champion at West Liberty State College in 1961, then transferred to Iowa State rival Oklahoma State as he chased an Olympic dream. A transplanted Iowa State graduate and Ames resident got the Douglas-Nichols connection started.

"I think there were a number of things that made me want to come to Iowa State as a high school wrestler. Number one, the history of wrestling at Iowa State. Also, Dr. Nichols was a national champion, and I thought he might be an excellent mentor for me because that was my goal…to be a national champion," Douglas said. "He had one of his alums by the name of Arthur Ruggles, and (Ruggles) saw me wrestle in high school and contacted Nichols. I guess he thought I was going to be a great wrestler. Nichols followed up and started recruiting me."

Douglas, an African American, grew up in poverty near the Ohio–West Virginia border.

"I would have never been able to get a coaching job had it not been for Dr. Harold Nichols. He helped me a great deal. Number one, he made sure that I stayed on top of my academics, and he gave me that opportunity while I was working with him," Douglas said. "He and I had some very interesting conversations. He told me (education) would really be important to me. You could win a national title, you could do all those things, but you get that master's degree so that you can teach and coach. That's the thing you will appreciate more than anything else. The fact that I got to be a schoolteacher, I'm forever grateful for that. I really, really love coaching, but I have a passion for teaching. I was an excellent health teacher, and I taught some history. I loved to see kids learn. I am who I am because of my education, not because of my wrestling ability. I will forever consider myself a good schoolteacher. My students tell me I was a good teacher, so I believe them."

Douglas remembered one exhaustive bus ride to Oklahoma State by way of Ames.

"Actually, on my way to Oklahoma State I stopped by Ames and watched them practice. I took a Greyhound bus from Wheeling, West Virginia, to someplace outside of Ames. I spent the night and watched them practice, and the next day I went on to Stillwater, Oklahoma," Douglas said. "I had a lot to think about. I wanted to be an Olympic champion, and I thought if I went to the right place and had the right people I could win that gold medal. That was my dream. But I had to leave not only my high school coach who was a good friend, but he was also like a father to me. I had to leave my future wife, Jackie, which wasn't easy to do, and I had to leave my friends, which wasn't easy to do, and I'd never been away from home. It was a tough, tough, tough decision I had to make, but I desired that gold medal so much that I couldn't say no. I had to go."

Trust was a challenge for Douglas, but not when it came to Nichols.

"Some of my neighbors were (Ku Klux) Klan members, and I was raised in a coal mining town. A lot of racism and a lot of racists, so I was always on guard. But I did trust Nick," Douglas affirmed. "He believed that all people were the same. He didn't believe in the difference in race; he truly believed that all people were the same, and he treated all people like that. He tried to make sure that his kids got a degree. In my opinion he never saw color. It's difficult to explain what kind of person he was because, as you remember, Harold Nichols didn't talk a whole lot. I spent some time riding with Harold Nichols on some of those trips, and we would have some very interesting conversations. You had to be careful when he was driving because he'd go to sleep, and one of the reasons we'd talk so much was because I wanted to make sure he wasn't going to fall asleep behind the wheel.

"I have never heard any black wrestler say anything negative about Harold Nichols. Sometimes he didn't do what they wanted him to do, but they still respected him. You can tell when somebody's a good person. Harold Nichols was a good person," Douglas said. "He was hell to compete against in the wrestling arena, but as a human being I considered Harold Nichols to be a friend. Even though we had some knock-down, drag-out battles and we had some disagreements, I always thought that he was a friend and I could respect him. He was a very special person."

Nichols's wife, Ruth, was a thoughtful woman whom Galea said could have easily lived in the most exclusive address in the country.

"Ruth Nichols could have easily been a First Lady," Galea said. "She was such a classy lady. Ruth Nichols sent my mother clippings, and my mother still speaks very highly about Nick and Ruth, but especially that Ruth would be considerate enough to send her things."

There was much to write about with Iowa State's wrestling program during the Nichols era. The Cyclones won a school record thirty-three-straight home meets between 1970 and 1974, and meets would draw as many as fifteen thousand fans. The Cyclone Wrestling Club was a support system for the team as well as those training for international competition, and the students were there at the ISU Armory or at Hilton Coliseum, which opened in December 1971.

"The biggest thing I remember is being acknowledged from being a wrestler at Iowa State, being a superstar. When I left campus and went out to work in the real world, I was a nobody. At Iowa State, I didn't want to leave. It was like your own little world there, and everybody loved wrestling there," Antonacci said. "To get the acknowledgement of a sport that's so tough, but it's a minor sport, you don't get the publicity like basketball players get or football players. At any other school that wouldn't have happened, but at Iowa State you are an elite athlete. You are acknowledged and appreciated, and that's something I just didn't want to go away. When I left, it was really difficult for me to adapt outside that environment."

Antonacci said it was important to Nichols that his wrestlers grow beyond mat skills during their time on campus. Antonacci said he came to Ames with a ninth-grade reading level at best. He worked with tutors and left with his name on the honor roll and a master's degree on his résumé.

"What I learned from Iowa State I've been doing in my own business for almost forty years," Antonacci said. "I was totally blessed that Nick and that program was there. Anywhere else, I wouldn't have made it. No way."

Antonacci also left Ames with a world record to his name. He broke a Guinness Book of World Records mark for most push-ups in thirty minutes on August 15, 1979, doing 1,630 at Beyer Hall. Previously, the record was held by a gentleman in Lancashire, England, who did 1,602. Antonacci's record grew from an original challenge for him to do 1,000 push-ups in the same time at a Pennsylvania wrestling camp. The next time, he did 1,200, and then he did 1,400.

"Nick wanted you to be the best you can be. He instilled an attitude in me which was, 'I want everybody on the team to get a pin, but I'm going to shoot for the fastest,'" Galea said. "In other words, a competition where everybody wins but you just do better than most. Les and Nick, between the two of them, they really instilled a winning attitude. My high school coach (Joe Campo) did that as well.

"I wanted to win all the time because I didn't want to disappoint Nick or anyone for that matter. There are some guys who were disappointed with certain things that happened, but from my standpoint it was an honor to wrestle for Nick and Les and work with Carl and Dale (Bahr) and the other coaches that came in. It's still such an important part of my life, I just can't get it out of my head how much I enjoyed being part of Iowa State wrestling. I wish I would have done better at certain times, but I can't tell you how much I really, really enjoyed it being there."

Adams had drawn up an idea for a wrestler's training tool that is still in use today. The product is known as "Adam" and is a dummy that helps a wrestler work on takedown technique.

"When I invented that 'Adam' takedown machine, I took him [Nichols] the drawing of it and told him I wanted to build a prototype," Adams said. "He said, 'Go ahead, I'll finance it,' and that's the only thing he said. That was the whole thing that allowed me to get that on the market, that Nick was going to finance it. Think about this: it speaks to the type of man he was and the relationships he built with his athletes. That was Nick."

Iowa State's program made headlines in publications like the *Predicament*, *National Mat News* or *Amateur Wrestling News* during the Nichols era, but Galea pulled off an amazing piece of recognition in the media back home when he won his fourth Big Eight Conference championship—a 12–0 victory over Kevin Young of Oklahoma. Galea's headshot was published next to that of tennis star Jimmy Connors on the back page of the *New York Times*. It might have gone unnoticed except someone called it to the attention of Galea's father that someone had the same last name as his. Dad looked and said, "Oh my goodness, that's my son,'" Pete recalled.

"Now how would I have gotten an opportunity for something like that if it wasn't for Nick?" Pete said.

Along with numerous big wins, Iowa State had the biggest loss when Larry Owings of Washington beat Gable 13–11 in the 142-pound championship match of the 1970 NCAA tournament. It was Gable's sole setback in high school or in college.

"To be honest, I think maybe it was probably one of the best things that could happen to the sport overall," Adams said, "because that put an exclamation point on the fact that on a given day, anyone could be beaten."

Iowa State's program got showers of printer's ink nearly three decades later as Cael Sanderson completed a 159-0 career with his fourth NCAA championship in 2002 at Albany, New York. Sanderson, one of four boys from Heber City, Utah, to wrestle for the Cyclones, became the second four-time winner in tournament history but the first to do it without a scuff. Sanderson was also named outstanding wrestler of the tournament an unprecedented four times. Sanderson lost one match as a true freshman when he was withheld from varsity competition, then started a big run.

"It was the biggest of all time. That is so hard to do," Adams said. "Gable almost did it, but he didn't. Pat Smith won four national championships, but he got beat along the way. John Smith got beat along the way although he was a six-time world champion. Cael got beat in freestyle after he graduated from college, but he ended up winning the Olympics. But to go through your collegiate career without ever losing a match is just unbelievable. In that regard, he's the best ever in my mind."

Two years later, Sanderson claimed the fifth gold medal by an Iowa State wrestler.

"I always felt that Sanderson amazed me because as a freshman he was at an upper weight and still clobbered people," Galea said. "That's pretty impressive. The awe of what he did is similar to the awe of Dan Gable."

Gable lost his final collegiate match to Larry Owings, but his legacy as the nation's best wrestler was already cemented. He further strengthened the legend by winning a gold medal in the 1972 Summer Olympics without giving up a point.

"There's no question about it, (Cael) was the greatest wrestler, I think, in NCAA history. But for some reason, there was an aura behind Gable that was very hard to beat as far as the magnificence of an athlete in wrestling,"

Galea said. "As much as I (see) Cael Sanderson as the greatest wrestler, I think Dan Gable's right up there with him. He had that one loss at the end.…Cael Sanderson, he just amazed me."

What if Gable and Sanderson hit their peak at the same time in the same weight class? "I also find myself comparing Gable and Cael. I wrestled with Gable, I worked out with Gable," Adams said. "If they were at the same weight, I don't know what would happen. In my mind, Gable was that tough. When I look at Cael, he was just as tough. It would have been a hell of a match, and I'm not willing to give either one of them the edge."

Douglas recruited the Sandersons to Iowa State: Cody, Cole, Cael and Cyler.

"I worked very hard at recruiting the Sanderson family. It wasn't a matter of trying to recruit Cael Sanderson—I had to recruit the whole family," Douglas said. "I spent time in Utah; they got to know me. You don't send three or four kids to a college without trusting the coach. They trusted me, and it's not easy to get people from that region to trust you."

Douglas saw big things, *magical things*, when Cael walked into the practice room.

"When you get a kid who's going to be 210–215 pounds and he's got the type of speed that a lightweight had, you've got something special. That was Cael," Douglas said. "There is no secret about his speed. There is no secret that that was a major factor in his success. The kids who competed against him, they had great match plans, but it's hard to plan for speed. We utilized that, and when he came through the door as a freshman, we started training him for the Olympic gold medal. There were some other guys who had the potential that Cael had, but Cael was a giant who moved like a lightweight. That type of speed and that type of ability, plus he had a tremendous competitive desire that was unique. You had to be around him in order to feel it and understand it.

"You'd have to see him in the wrestling room when we're in combat mode; you'd have to see him on the track when we're in training mode. You'd have to see him on that treadmill. Once you saw him on that treadmill, you'd get a good idea this guy's going to be special," Douglas said. "He used to make the treadmill literally cry. I would catch him on that treadmill, I'd hear the treadmill, I'd open the door and he'd be blasting that treadmill. The treadmill would be screaming, and I'd close the door and not go in because I didn't want to disturb him. I said to myself, 'There's no way anybody's going to beat this guy.' He treated that treadmill like a stepchild."

Sanderson often had a string of takedowns in a match, much like he desired a string of fish when he broke out his rod and reel. Only two opponents, Vertus Jones of West Virginia and Damion Hahn of Minnesota, lost to him by one point. Cael was a rare individual in the sport, much like some a generation before him.

"Guys like Dan Gable come around every so often. Guys like Dan Hodge, Tommy Evans, Myron Roderick…and I'm stepping back into history. Those guys, there was something very special about them. Cael Sanderson is in that crowd, and maybe the top of the class. There has never been a big man move as fast as Cael Sanderson," Douglas said. "I saw some of the fastest wrestlers on earth. Most of them were from Japan. Yojiro Uetake Obata, fast. (Osamu) Watanabe, fast. I start looking back at some of those Japanese superstars, and I wrestled them, I know how fast they were. I don't care how much strength you have or what kind of desire and drive you have; you can't teach speed. If you've got it and you learn how to use it, you can be special."

Adams said Nichols facilitated a lot of special things at a school that has been a part of many noteworthy events through the years.

"It's not Iowa and it's not Oklahoma State, but you have to have pioneers to get things going, particularly in the state of Iowa. Iowa State was a pioneer. Iowa State spawned Gable; Iowa State spawned Cael Sanderson," Adams asserted. "One way to look at it is a lot of the great things that have happened in the sport of wrestling were spawned by Iowa State and spawned by Coach Harold Nichols.

"When you look at Harold Nichols, a lot of coaches coach, but Nick had the biggest camps in the country. He put together a system of camps that a lot of people copied. Nick had his own equipment company. He used to manufacture wrestling gear," Adams said. "He was the one who came out with those robes, and a lot of people want Iowa State to bring them back. A lot of what's happening in wrestling, even in regard to rules. Nick was a leader, and when he spoke other coaches listened."

5
NORTHERN IOWA

The college wrestling program in Cedar Falls, Iowa, made bold headlines by winning the 1950 NCAA championship as Iowa State Teachers College.

Charles "Chuck" Patten watched Coach Dave McCuskey and the Panthers crown three individual champions in that tournament at the school's venerable West Gymnasium. Perhaps a how-to seed was planted in Patten's mind that day, waiting twenty-five years to sprout its own golden harvest when he was coaching at his alma mater, now known as University of Northern Iowa.

Perhaps Patten got to the gym five minutes before the action started. Maybe he stayed five minutes after it was done.

The school has been known as Iowa State Teachers College, State College of Iowa and University of Northern Iowa, but the Panthers' wrestling program has been known primarily for its tough individuals making a mark on the national and international scene.

Bill Smith of Council Bluffs Jefferson never won a state championship in high school but won two NCAA championships and a gold medal in the 1952 Olympics. Drew Foster of Mediapolis became the talk of the 2019 NCAA tournament by winning the 184-pound championship after a best finish of second in the state tournament. Gerald "Germ" Leeman of Osage was a silver medalist in the 1948 Olympics, and Maynard Harmon of Sac City, Koll and Bill Nelson of Eagle Grove were also Olympians. Nelson, Koll and Keith Young of Algona were three-time NCAA champions, as were Gary Bentrim of Cedar Rapids Jefferson and Kirk Myers of Algona in

NCAA Division II. Dave McCuskey coached the program to the 1950 championship, Patten led the charge in 1975 and 1978 and the Panthers have finished among the top ten teams in thirty-six national tournaments. They had an overall mark of 772-428-28 going into their ninety-fifth season in the 2019–20 schedule.

Patten had his only losing season (4-9-1) in his debut campaign—the place was known as State College of Iowa then—and built a program that claimed two NCAA Division II championships. In each championship effort, the Panthers had three individual champions among the team's ten qualifiers.

The leader of those teams was a soft-spoken man with a touch of self-deprecating wit in a sport full of demonstrative, highly vocal coaches. Patten could illuminate the technical aspect of winning, but he had the special touch of getting to the mental game with an individual and making big winners out of those who might have been passed over by bigger programs for scholarships because they lacked the large collection of high school gold medals. He was "C.P." to virtually anyone who met him.

Chuck Patten led his alma mater, University of Northern Iowa, to NCAA Division II team championships in 1975 and in 1978. He was in the stands in UNI's West Gym when the Panthers won their first title in 1950. Patten is best known as "C.P." by his coaches, wrestlers and thousands of friends. *Photo by Dan McCool.*

"I think he had a tendency to be able to help you achieve at a level you didn't think you could. You were better walking out of that place than you were walking in, in *every* way," said two-time NCAA Division II champion Jim Miller, who later led Wartburg to ten NCAA Division III team titles. "He created character as a part of the program. When you've got great character and you're willing to do things, compete—not just for yourself but for your teammates—I think you get a better result. He was great at that."

Miller was never a state champion at Waterloo East High School—Patten medaled but never struck gold for East—but he was one of twelve Iowans who totaled twenty national championships for Patten.

Another Iowan who was a national champion at UNI, Keith Poolman of Clarion, said Patten had a different touch as a coach, which included teaching *everyone* on the team how to win. "C.P. just took everybody under his wing," Poolman said. "Here's another thing I really respect about him: He had a ladder board, you have your No. 1 who wrestled varsity and you had your No. 4, 5 or 6 down the line. It didn't matter who it was, he was there for you. If somebody wanted to learn, he would take you and teach you."

In some cases, Patten would find you. Poolman remembered Patten recruited a one-time state champion from Algona named Kirk Myers. As a result, the Panthers got a three-time Division II national champion who also placed three times in the Division I meet in the time when select wrestlers from Division II and Division III got to compete with the big boys. Myers and Gary Bentrim were three-time champions for Patten.

"The thing that we always said was, 'You do what it takes in the practice room, and the results will show on the mat.' That's kind of what (C.P.'s) philosophy was," Poolman said. "For example, he recruited Kirk Myers. Never wrestled varsity until his senior year and won the state tournament. No one even knew him, (C.P.) was the only one who recruited him, and he ended up becoming a six-time all-American. He definitely saw somebody that was something else."

Poolman said the base of Patten's work was his belief in the wrestler as a person and his willingness to let the wrestler know that. Then he taught the wrestler to believe in himself by working hard and doing the little things. Sometimes the work was done five minutes before practice and five minutes after practice.

"If you lost a match because of a guy cradling you, boom, five minutes before practice, five minutes after practice for a week or two and guess what, you never got cradled again," Poolman said. "He was a philosopher, and when he talked he had a way of talking *with* us, not *to* us. It wasn't like he made us do things that we didn't want to do. We did them because we knew he had our best interest at heart. We knew that was going to make us better; we knew that was going to make us win more. That was the thing I saw when I came in as a freshman. I lost my first tryout to (Dick) Erickson, who was second in the nation the year before. I'm walking out of the room, and (Patten) goes, 'You want me to teach you how to beat him?' I didn't know who he was talking to. I looked back, and no one else was around. I said, 'Who are you talking to? This guy just got second in the nation with you. Why would you teach me how to beat him?' (Patten said), 'Do you want to know how to beat him?' I said, 'Yes.' Five minutes before practice, five minutes after."

It also helped to have a champion as a tutor, Poolman said.

"Jim Miller was one of the guys who took me under his wing. He took me in the room and said, 'Let's work out.' And he said, 'Take a shot.' Every time I took a shot, boom, I'm on my face," Poolman said. "He's got two. So he gets up again, and I said, 'I can do this.' I take a shot, I'm on my face, he's got two. I was like, 'I don't even see you move, how [are] you doing that?' All he did was move his hands two inches up. I would fake, and he would have two. I walked out of the room and said, 'Oh my gosh, I have so much to learn. Let's start right now.' And I said, 'Show me what you're doing.' It was unreal, and they took us under their wing and taught us all that stuff. Jim Miller was amazing."

Poolman had a long career as a college and high school wrestling referee. He still does some college work but does a lot of supervising and mentoring with younger officials. Patten's teaching methods have found their way into Poolman's educating those on the whistle.

"The years I wrestled under C.P. and the things he taught us—and I still use them in officiating, too—it's the little things you do as an official that makes you better too," Poolman said. "Chuck taught us a lot. I'll never remember the big move he taught us, but the little things like your wrist out, elbows in....I'll always remember those things because those are the little things that kept me from going to my belly."

An early insight into how Patten might have a different approach to the student-athlete came in a July 1964 article from the *Waterloo Courier* after Patten had been hired in Cedar Falls.

"I'm going to do nothing the next couple of months but go around and visit boys and try to talk them into going on to school—any school," he was quoted. "I just want to see them get an education. I'm a little late, I suppose. Most of this year's graduates already have made up their mind so I'm going to start working on the sophomores and juniors...urge them to get their grades up and start thinking about college."

Don Briggs, who replaced Patten after serving as his graduate assistant and then assistant coach, said he remembered Patten working often with psychologist Dave Whitsett.

"He studied these guys as we brought them in just to see what made them tick, what turned them on, what turned them off. I'll never forget (Whitsett) was trying to teach Chuck and myself how to teach a wrestler a move," Briggs said. "We had to ask (the wrestler) questions like, 'How many windows did you have in your house that you grew up in?' If the guy's eyes went up before he gave an answer, that meant you taught him verbally. If they went to the side or down, that meant you taught them visually. If they just looked straight at you, then you taught them physically, getting them to feel the move. That's just one example of a lot of the things that C.P. did, learned from Whitsett and other things like past experiences."

Patten would never consider himself great as a wrestler, even though he made three trips to the NCAA tournament while wrestling for Bill Koll, a three-time NCAA champion and tournament outstanding wrestler for the Panthers.

"It was kind of a matter of not being a very good athlete myself but having real good competition in the room to beat me around a little bit," Patten said. "I think, when that happens, you either get better or you quit. Not very many guys stayed the same."

Patten said early lessons were in the cards for him at college.

"First year, freshmen weren't eligible so I learned how to play double-deck pinochle in the off-campus lounge with all the guys coming back from the DEW (distant early warning) line up in northern Canada who had been monitoring the radar for Cold War possible invasion of America," Patten said.

The squad in Cedar Falls was composed of mostly guys who loved wrestling or who wanted to coach. "Iowa is a great wrestling state, but we didn't have a lot of athletes. Bill didn't recruit athletes. He didn't recruit at all, in fact," Patten said. "He didn't recruit me. I didn't want to go in the military, and I didn't want to work construction. I didn't have any skills, so I went across the town to Iowa State Teachers College because Bill Gardner, one of my high school friends and teammates, lived near me and we were going to drive over and go to school."

After completing his eligibility, Patten set out as a teacher and coach who won a wrestling state championship in California and in Oregon prior to answering what would be a life-changing phone call from his alma mater. As he worked on a graduate degree, Patten also served as freshman coach for the 1961–62 season at University of Oregon.

"Jim Witham was the athletic director at the time. The fact that I could play golf *and* coach wrestling and had a master's degree made that feasible to call me, I guess," Patten said. "When he (called), I couldn't believe it, but I took the job and I probably shouldn't have because I was way too young and not really as successful as a coach.... The wins and losses aren't what coaching's about. It's the other part that helps, and after a couple of years

I realized Xs and Os—if you can call technique Xs and Os—are pretty easy, but knowing when to hug a guy and when to kick him in the rear is what coaching's about. How you handle individuals. That took me a long time. I started to get the drift of it about the time I needed to quit for health reasons."

Patten said the program began to accrue its success in earnest when Miller (Waterloo East) and Ken Snyder (Waterloo Columbus) came across town as he did. Also, Randy Omvig had come to school from Eagle Grove and Briggs was hired as a graduate assistant.

"So, we had good kids and they worked out with each other all the time," Patten said. "Dave Cunningham was good enough to go with anybody in the country. (He) beat Dave Haines from Wisconsin (two-time national champion). He was as good as anybody, Milboy was as good as anybody, (Snyder) was as good as anybody, Omvig was as good...so if you could put a couple of other people with them, you got a chance to place."

Patten did well recruiting guys who weren't highly decorated in high school. Poolman was a two-time finalist in high school; Miller was third. Snyder and Omvig each won state once.

"A lot of those kids still had a fire in their belly. Miller and Snyder were really the answer. I remember talking to them after their freshman year. One of them was like 2-8 and the other guy was 5-5," Patten recalled. "I called them into the office and said, 'You guys get ready because you're going to be the heart and soul of this program the next four years. You need to hear what and how this was going to take place.' You could see the success Jim Miller had as a coach at Wartburg. The fire was there, the coaching was there, the personality was there. So, I guess I made a good decision with those two. Snyder same way with investing and finances he went into. He's been very successful."

In those days, the NCAA Division II tournament was a bear of a competition, and a team needed more than just a couple studs to figure into the team race. A good number of quality wrestlers were necessary to deal with strong squads such as Cal Poly–San Luis Obispo, Clarion of Pennsylvania and Portland State. Patten said thinking seriously about a team championship had some roots in the 1970 tournament. Northern Iowa took a ten-man contingent to the tournament in Ohio, but the Panthers had five still going on the second day: 167-pound finalist Skip Bellock and Marv Reiland at 134, Clint Young at 158, Bob Boeck at 177 and Mike McCready at heavyweight in the consolation bracket. Bellock lost a one-point decision, but the "consy" quartet won ten of twelve matches and Northern Iowa finished second to perennial power Cal Poly.

"That made me realize that some things were working out OK, and maybe if I could learn how to coach, as those guys all called me...they were my guinea pigs when I was learning how," Patten said. "It became a goal or an obsession to say, 'We can win this thing.'"

Since tying Upper Iowa for eighth place in 1968, Northern Iowa was a top-four finisher in five of the next six national tournaments. Three of the finishes were second place in 1970, 1972 and 1974.

Patten was close to missing the 1975 fruit of his labor at Northern Iowa. An article in the April 18, 1974 edition of the Jefferson City *Capital News* stated Patten was offered the wrestling coach position at University of Missouri, but he turned it down to remain in Cedar Falls. Patten said William Thrall, head of Northern Iowa's physical education department at the time, asked him not to take the offer until the Panthers could put together a counteroffer to keep him. Part of the deal was making Briggs an assistant coach for the Panthers, albeit for not much money. Briggs said one aspect made it all worthwhile.

"Just him, I guess. There wasn't anything to dislike," Briggs said. "It gave me responsibility, it made me feel like I was beneficial to the success that we had, and we shared that."

Briggs said Patten had the coaching goods to win in Cedar Falls, Columbia, Missouri, or anywhere else he might have landed. But the time when a move to Missouri seemed a sure bet was unsettling, Briggs said.

"I remember that time, and I remember it was like, 'Whoa, this is scary.' He and I were both in love with our wrestlers. How do you leave them? Who's going to want to go with us?" Briggs said. "He would have been able to make the adjustments from the UNI wrestlers to the Missouri wrestlers. Missouri wasn't a powerhouse in wrestling at the time, so obviously there was room for growth and room for improvement. I think he's a great coach no matter where he would go."

Patten said Briggs was valuable because he'd learned a lot of what Patten wanted in recruits. The wrestlers seconded their coach's wishes. Briggs said one recruiting visit to campus was cut short because the wrestlers told Patten the individual was likely not going to be a good fit for the program.

"(Briggs) was instrumental in everything that happened during my reign there because he knew me and he recruited guys that he knew I could tolerate," Patten said. "I just can't abide guys who don't care about rules or regulations, don't have integrity. Winning at all costs is not my game at all."

Briggs laughed as he brought up how he and Patten often thought alike. One instance was the time Briggs had a late-night inspiration of how it would be cool to have a "booster of the meet" award at dual meets. He wrote it down so he'd not forget to bring it up to Patten. The next morning, Briggs said he told Patten of a great idea he'd thought up for meets, but Patten said he wanted to bring up an idea he'd been considering: why not have a booster of the meet?

"I didn't feel like an assistant coach to him. I felt like a brother, a son even," Briggs said. "He made not only me but the wrestlers and everybody else feel the same way. It was a family to him."

Patten didn't like individuals not being team players. Poolman learned about that early in his time at Northern Iowa.

"C.P. was a stickler for rules: You don't miss practice; you move mats when everybody's supposed to move mats. One time as a freshman I skipped mats, and he didn't let me practice for three days," Poolman said. "It was the worst three days of my life. That affected me more than anything else. He said if you don't want to be a part of the team, then guess what, you're not going to work out either. That was the biggest effect on me as a freshman that I can ever remember. I never missed a thing after that. Not one. Not even close."

Poolman said he had offers from Iowa and Iowa State (Cyclone coach Harold Nichols visited him, but after Poolman had signed), but Patten's blunt assessment of what could be made Poolman feel as though he'd found a home on his recruiting visit.

"He didn't mince any words. He wasn't like 'Wow, you can do this, you can do that.' He said, 'If you don't work hard, if you don't do the things we ask you to, if you don't listen, you won't make it,'" Poolman recalled. "Then you talk to the guys who had been wrestling for him for a year like Jim Miller and Ken Snyder, (Randy) Omvig…those guys all said, 'You'll never get a better technique coach than Chuck Patten.' It was a plan definitely made in Heaven. I'll always be blessed because I chose UNI and Chuck Patten, there's no doubt about it. It was the little things he taught us that were the big things in the match."

The 1978 championship, just like the 1950 trophy, was won in Cedar Falls. Patten said the thought was 1978 might be a second consecutive title.

"I thought we'd win it in '77. We hosted the nationals in '77 as well. I thought we had the best team," Patten said. "Ed Hermann, our 190-pounder, got sick and we didn't get anything out of him. He was the best guy in the country, I thought, and everybody who saw him thought that, too. That cost us 16–20 points and we ended up (third)."

Cal State–Bakersfield won with $107\frac{1}{4}$ points, and Augustana of South Dakota was second with 78. Northern Iowa finished with $74\frac{3}{4}$ points.

"The next year we lost (Gary) Bentrim in early September to a shoulder injury…but he came back right before the tournament and ended up winning it at 158 instead of 142. We probably should have taken him at 150 but I would have had to bump a four-year guy off of 150 and I wouldn't do that."

Northern Iowa's championship seasons took place during the time Iowa coach Dan Gable was the one for college recruits and their plans. Patten said he recruited some major talent hard, but a phone call from Gable often ended the prospect of someone wearing purple and gold. What Patten had was a gang of guys with fire in the belly.

"Think back to the time and think of the phenomena that had taken place. I call it the Gable phenomena. Dan Gable was such an icon in wrestling. Not just in Iowa—especially in Iowa—but all over the country. Every kid wanted to be touched by Dan Gable," Patten said. "They would go to Iowa even though they weren't recruited. We recruited Barry Davis from the time he was a freshman all the way until a week before…. We had him until a week before the signing date. Gable called him, and he went to Iowa. You go back to the old adage you don't run Shetland ponies in the Kentucky Derby. You may not win it, but if you can get guys who still have a fire and you get enough of an attitude around you in your room and in your program, they'll drag other guys with them and pretty soon you're competitive on a national level, so that is kind of what happened."

What Patten was able to direct at State College of Iowa/Northern Iowa was impressive when numbers came into play. Schools such as Iowa and Iowa State had gigantic operating budgets. Northern Iowa's budget fit on a shoestring. Patten called himself a "professional beggar."

"I had to run around with my hand out," Patten said. "My budget when I got there in 1964–65 was $7,800. My budget when I left eighteen years later was $10,000, and that was to pay for referees, travel, transportation, food…"

A little psychology came into play around tournament time, Patten said.

"They read the paper, too, so you try to do and say things that will get them to be the best they can be," Patten said. "You don't have to be the best guy in the country, you just have to be the best the weekend they hold the tournament."

Poolman remembered Patten getting the value of always working hard in practice through to his wrestlers.

"The biggest thing is if you do it in practice, you're going to do it in a meet, and that is a philosophy of Chuck Patten," Poolman said. "By gosh, it was absolutely true. I totally remember this that I said, 'Aww, I'm going to take it a little easier in practice' so I laid on my belly. My God, in the meet I found myself doing the same thing."

"We found ourselves listening to Chuck because the things he told us worked so well. It wasn't any big, big thing. He would never show us throws; he would never show us the big move to pin the guy. It was always how you point your fingers, you keep your fingers together? Where do you put your elbows? How do you stand in your stance? How do you take a shot? I always tell people this: Chuck Patten coached Jim Miller, Jim Miller coached Nick Mitchell, now Nick Mitchell is coaching a lot of guys and passing it down, too."

The trio of Patten, Miller and Mitchell have combined for twenty national team championships going into the 2019–20 season.

Briggs remembered Patten always looking for a way to get the most out of every teaching moment, even between periods or when the wrestlers run out of usable room in a match.

"I remember we had many talks about when you're wrestling and go off the mat, he wanted you to immediately turn and look at him so he'd give either sign language or give you an indication of what he wanted you to do," Briggs said. "Maybe it was verbally. He said, 'I don't need to yell your name, I don't need to yell to get your attention because that takes time. When you go off the mat, just look over. That's all I'm asking you to do.' Guys would do that. He knew and studied wrestling inside and out and knew what to communicate to the wrestler. That's how he got across to them."

Briggs also remembered the feeling of being able to hoist the championship trophy in 1975 and 1978.

"In one sense you could see it coming because we knew we were a pretty good team both of those years," Briggs said. "It was like, 'Hold your breath, hold your breath, ahhh, we got it. Yes.'"

Patten was forty-three when he resigned as head coach after the 1981–82 season. After starting the program as a Division I entity, he moved into Northern Iowa's athletic administration as assistant to the athletic director. Briggs was immediately named as his successor. Patten would later leave the Panthers for an administrative position in education in the state of Washington.

"I divorced myself from it, then knew I had to get away from here so Briggs could run free spirit," Patten said, adding he had thoughts he'd be at Northern Iowa forever.

Briggs said he found the value of his years of working with Patten after he stepped into Patten's old job.

"That helped me immensely. I can't tell you how many times I was like, 'What would C.P. do in this situation?' when I became a head coach. To see it through his eyes, it was a lot easier being an assistant coach than it was a head coach. Being able to sit back and see things through his eyes really helped me in a lot of ways," Briggs said. "Without the experience of working with him, I wouldn't have been able to handle a lot of the things. He just had a way of, 'Don't make this a knee-jerk reaction, let's think about this a little bit and then come up with a solution.'"

Patten was asked nearly forty years after he stepped down what he remembered about his time as Northern Iowa's wrestling coach.

"It's almost like it didn't happen. You're thousands of miles away, and wrestling is very low-key in the West Coast. We don't get results of the national championship, let alone the teams or individuals. So, I stay in touch with it through technology today," Patten said. "I wouldn't be who I am if I wouldn't have had the opportunity. It helped me more than it helped UNI. I grew a lot as a person and kind of formulated a philosophy of life and the way you treat people. It's part of the reason why the president upsets the hell out of me today, because he doesn't treat people the way I think you should treat people."

Mike Allen of Waterloo was the first African American referee to work the state wrestling tournament. Allen was a highly respected official for high school and college meets, then became a supervisor of officials for the Big Ten Conference and the Big 12 Conference. *Photo by Dan McCool.*

Briggs, Mark Manning, Brad Penrith and now Doug Schwab have followed Patten as Northern Iowa's coach. Patten sees big things possible for Schwab, who coached his first individual national champion in Drew Foster in 2019.

"Doug will get some of those guys, and when he does he'll coach them. When he's done coaching them, they'll be successful, and UNI will be a name to be reckoned with," Patten said. "Probably the only sport that really can be a national champion at the Division I level at a UNI kind of school."

The NCAA took a three-year break from its wrestling tournament because of World War II after the 1942 event at Michigan State. Beginning with the 1946 tournament, Iowa State Teachers College made its move toward the top with Coach Dave McCuskey. The wrestlers loved McCuskey and held reunions at NCAA tournaments decades later, celebrating their time as "Mac's Boys."

The 1950 championship may have been born out of frustration in the previous four tournaments. Iowa State Teachers College placed second in 1946, 1947 and 1949 and tied Purdue and Iowa for fourth in 1948. During that quadrennial, the Panthers scored thirteen individual national championships.

What is now known as West Gym on the Cedar Falls campus played host to the 1950 tournament. Iowa State Teachers College brought an all-Iowa lineup into the fray and walked away as team champion, 14 points ahead of Purdue. Keith Young of Algona, Bill Nelson of Eagle Grove and Bill Smith of Council Bluffs Jefferson were national champions. Floyd Oglesby of Mason City and Fred Stoeker of Keystone were runners-up.

Along with five finalists, the Panthers had a third-place finish from 121-pounder Frank Altman and a fourth-place showing from Luverne Klar at 128. They were both from R.D. Mitchell's Osage program. The only non-placer was 175-pounder Max Long of Missouri Valley. Long was the first of two Missouri Valley wrestlers to compete in the NCAA Division I tournament, the other being Dalton Jensen of Iowa State in 2010.

Notable about the 1950 tournament were some of the names ISTC guys crossed paths with. Altman's only loss at 121 pounds that weekend, 7–6, was to Tony Gizoni of Waynesburg, who was selected as outstanding wrestler of the tournament. Altman beat future Michigan State coach Grady Peninger, then wrestling for Oklahoma State, in a 2–0 contest.

Klar dropped a 3–2 match against eventual champion Joe Patacsil of Purdue at 128. In the consolation, Klar lost the third-place bout to Jack Blubaugh of Oklahoma. Blubaugh was a Pan American Games gold medalist in 1955 and is the brother of 1960 Summer Olympic gold medalist Doug Blubaugh.

Patacsil's grandson Jake Patacsil was a third-generation wrestler at Purdue and an all-American who later served as an assistant coach at Central College in Pella.

Oglesby was familiar with referee's decision matches at 136 pounds. He won such a contest in the quarterfinals en route to a finals showdown with Cornell College star Lowell Lange of Waterloo. Lange won a 2–2, referee's decision to collect his second consecutive championship. Lange beat Leon Wayne Smith of Fort Dodge, wrestling for Navy, in the semifinals. Smith finished third with a victory over Charles Farina of Purdue. Farina's son Mike was a member of the 1976 Olympic Greco-Roman team and wrestled at Iowa State.

Nelson and Ken Hunte of Syracuse met in the 155-pound finals for the second year in a row. Nelson had an 8–1 victory in this meeting. Hunte's son Steve Hunte was a member of three NCAA championship teams at University of Iowa.

Young won three matches, including a referee's decision in the semifinals, to win, 5–2, over Charles Moreno of Purdue in the 145-pound finals. Smith, a future Olympic champion, beat James LaRock of Ithaca 10–7 in the 165-pound finale.

Stoeker is a footnote in NCAA history, losing to three-time heavyweight champion Dick Hutton of Oklahoma State. Hutton was a four-time finalist, the first to accomplish that until Lee Kemp of Wisconsin in 1978. Had he not lost to Verne Gagne of Minnesota in the 1949 finals—Hutton's lone loss in college—he would have beaten Pat Smith of Oklahoma State by forty-four years to the punch of being the first four-time NCAA champion.

The Lange-Oglesby-Smith finish as the top three at 136 pounds is the only time three Iowans were at the top of a weight class in the Division I tournament. It was one of nine times that two products of Iowa's high schools met in the D-1 finals. Going into the 2019–20 season, the most recent occasion was 2010, when Matt McDonough of Iowa and Linn-Mar of Marion beat Andrew Long of Iowa State and Creston/Orient-Macksburg's program at 125 pounds.

6
WARTBURG

Jim Miller began exploring NCAA Division I head coaching positions as he finished his sixth season as an assistant coach at University of Northern Iowa in Cedar Falls. One drawback to such a promotion was selling his family on a move to a new community.

"I wanted to be a head wrestling coach. I was looking only at D-1 schools at that time," said Miller, who was born James Melton Miller but is better known by his nickname, Milboy, a moniker given to him by one of his coaches at Waterloo East High School, NCAA champion Bill Dotson.

Tragically, Wartburg College in Waverly was seeking a wrestling coach. The NCAA Division III school fifteen miles north of Cedar Falls lost its longtime coach, Dick Walker, in an automobile accident on September 10, 1990. Walker, who was beginning his twenty-third year at the school, had twice led the Knights to Iowa Conference championships. His record was 180-93-4, and Walker was a three-time choice as Iowa Conference "Coach of the Year." His devotion to the conference and the respect seemingly everyone had for him were reasons why the league—now known as the American Rivers Conference—affixed Walker's name to the Coach of the Year honor.

Wartburg had gotten Bob Siddens to come out of retirement and serve as interim head coach for the 1990–91 season. Wartburg placed fourth in the 1991 conference tournament and twelfth in the NCAA meet. Miller was announced as Wartburg's new coach at the beginning of March 1991, just before he helped the Panthers win their sixth consecutive West Region

Eric Keller watches a Wartburg College wrestler during a match. Keller was an assistant to Wartburg coach Jim Miller, they served as co-head coaches and Keller took the top job when Miller retired. Keller has led the Knights to four NCAA Division III national championships. He and Miller won three titles as co-head coaches. *Photo by Dan McCool.*

championship and then have three all-Americans in placing tenth in the NCAA tournament.

Walker had served as an assistant under Siddens at Waterloo West High School for six seasons prior to leaving for the college coaching ranks. Siddens was a Hall of Fame coach who led the Wahawks to ten state championships and coached an undefeated, three-time state champion named Dan Gable at West.

The Miller era began with seven returning veterans, including all-Americans Tom Hogan and Jon Dawley. Wartburg opened on November 14 with a 24–16 victory over Buena Vista. The Knights, who finished the NCAA meet tied with Ithaca and Wisconsin–Stevens Point for eighth place, were soon a team to watch in a state where NCAA Division I's Iowa, Iowa State and Northern Iowa commanded much of the attention.

The Iowa Conference tournament championship round became so good—even with Wartburg piling up the team title—that Iowa Public Television would televise it live. That was one of the few non–Division I meets shown on the series. Another was the clash between Wartburg and Augsburg of Minneapolis in what is known as the "Battle of the Burgs."

Since 1995, either Wartburg or Augsburg has won the national Division III team title. Wartburg has fourteen national titles; Augsburg won its thirteenth in 2019.

Joe Breitbach was a Waterloo East graduate and a former Wartburg wrestler. A local business owner, Breitbach is close enough to the program that he could be thought of as a coach. He *is* certified as a coach. In Milboyspeak, he's an "E'loo guy." They crossed paths one night, and Breitbach brought up the Wartburg job.

"I just happened to run into him, and I said, 'This looks like it would be a good thing. I think it would be a good fit for you,'" Breitbach recalled. "The East Waterloo deal was part of it, but more than that I just knew that Jimmy was probably a better coach as far as fundamentals and stuff and did it the right way. He was sort of spinning his wheels down there at UNI because he wasn't the (head coach). He was doing a good job, but he wasn't calling the shots."

Miller found himself in a proverbial tight spot. As the top assistant to Don Briggs at UNI, he was recruiting talent to the school, and the newest crop was early in its time at school.

"The situation ended up that being the type of guy he is, he got back to me and said, 'Joe, I appreciate you thinking about me, but I've got kids

Jim Miller had a desire to be an NCAA Division I head wrestling coach. Fellow Waterloo East High School graduate Joe Breitbach (*left*) got Miller to look at the head coaching job at NCAA Division III Wartburg College. The result? Miller led Wartburg to ten national team titles. *Photo by Dan McCool.*

that I recruited, they're in-house already and I couldn't do that to Briggs,'" Breitbach recalled. "That's the kind of stand-up guy Coach Miller is. He said, 'I can't do it now, but I certainly would like to be considered if there is some way it's delayed or whatever.'"

The "whatever" came in a group effort.

"Coincidentally, that next week I came home from work and my kids—I had a thirteen-year-old, a twelve-year-old and a six-year-old—and they were sitting on the couch with my wife, which was really weird," Miller said. "I go, 'What's going on here?' They go, 'Dad, we're not moving.' They had made some kind of a deal. That's when I said maybe I should really look at Wartburg because it's fifteen miles up the road. We can stay; we did stay. Matter of fact, I'm still living in the same house thirty-some years later."

Miller's coaching performance at Wartburg earned him another home—the NCAA Division III Hall of Fame. He led the Knights to 10 team championships as either head coach or co-head coach with Eric Keller. The Knights won 7 Duals championships, earning a 413-37-2 record in dual meets and 21 consecutive conference tournament titles. The fan base that followed Wartburg was known as "Milboy's Army." Under Miller's direction, Wartburg started two streaks that remained active going into the 2019–20 season: 213 victories over conference foes and 27 conference championships.

Wartburg had an amazing eight-year run of finishing either first or second in the Division III national tournaments—twenty-one of twenty-three years dating back to 1996—halted in 2019 with a sixth-place finish. The Miller name was still in play, even though Jim retired after the 2012–13 season. Loras College in Dubuque placed a program-best second. Its head coach is T.J. Miller, Jim Miller's son, or "Milboy's boy" to the longtime Miller followers.

The Knights' sixth-place finish in 2019 was their lowest since 2001, the last time a conference school finished ahead of Wartburg. That year, Luther College of Decorah finished fourth. The 2019 tournament was the first time since 2002 that Wartburg failed to have an individual national finalist or crown a national champion.

Had Breitbach not put the Wartburg idea in Miller's head that night, who knows where the program was headed? If then athletic director John Kurtt followed a concern he had, Miller might have found that Division I job he wanted.

"Kurtt ran into the same thing; all the good guys were working, and they were committed to their season. He pulled the rabbit out and got

Siddens to come out of retirement for a year, and with the help of the Walker brothers, they turned in a respectable year," Breitbach said. "That was long before we were good, and it didn't take long after Coach Miller arrived that we were good."

The Walker brothers were Dick's sons, Steve and Matt, who had been Wartburg wrestlers and then assistants to their dad.

Breitbach said he had done some lobbying on Miller's behalf to get his friend an interview.

"(Miller) got an interview with our athletic director, and I spoke with John Kurtt afterwards," Breitbach said. "I said, 'How did Milboy look to you? As good as I told you he was going to be?' He said, 'Joe, everything you said was good, but he's sort of got a wild look in his eye.' I said, '*Hire him. That's what you want.*' He was worried about that wild look. It was a change in culture from what we'd had before, but obviously within two years the results were on the mat and it hasn't changed since."

Miller added, "What happened there was pretty incredible really, when you look at history, and I was proud to be a part of it."

It could have changed through the years, and Miller could have needed to broach the idea of moving to the family once again. But the coach and the community fell for each other.

The *Waterloo Courier* had a preview article of Miller's first season at Wartburg on November 10, 1991. One comment spoke volumes about Miller's desires and his patience level: "I'd like Wartburg to be a national title contender somewhere down the line, and the faster we get there the better."

Five years later, the Knights were celebrating the first national championship trophy in school history and in Iowa Conference history.

"I just felt like why couldn't we win a national championship on that level?" Miller said. "I didn't know how long it would take. It was a rough start because the first year we couldn't even fill the team. We were forfeiting a weight. I didn't know that it would happen as fast as it did. I put my head down and went to work *hard*, and good things started to happen. By golly, we ended up being the top team in America to that point. It was a heck of a ride, a journey. It was a real good decision that I made at that point."

Division III programs such as Wartburg do not offer athletic scholarships like their Division I and Division II cousins do, so the likelihood of Miller amassing a room full of three- and four-time state champions was implausible. However, Miller was a two-time national Division II champion and NCAA Division I runner-up as a four-time all-American at Northern Iowa—the Panthers were coached at that time by another E'loo guy, Chuck

Patten—after finishing no better than third in the Iowa state high school tournament. He knew hard work could do big things, and he liked recruiting similar wrestlers to campus.

"Changing the culture is hard no matter where you're at and what you're doing, but things started to get better. Some of the things go right back to Chuck Patten at UNI. I was starting to recruit character and hard workers, not just talent. Talent was not the top thing on the list," Miller said. "We were looking for hardworking kids, kids that knew how to fight, kids that really wanted to be good. I (was) looking for those kids that maybe weren't the blue-chip kids or didn't finish the way they wanted, but they had a burning desire to succeed. Man, that's who we were looking for. When you get that kind of culture going in your room, everybody's level started to raise. I know our culture started raising the level of everybody, not just physically but mentally. We liked it, everybody liked it and all of a sudden we're sitting there with a chance to win a championship."

One of those hungry, hardworking kids was LeRoy Gardner III, who wrestled at Hastings High School in Minnesota. Gardner's coach, Al Price, had been a graduate assistant at UNI when Miller was coaching there.

"I really wanted to go to a place where I thought more people thought and felt like I did about wrestling, and wanted to give themselves to it 100 percent," Gardner said. "After Wartburg won it in 1999, which was my senior year in high school, it definitely popped up on the radar. I was like, 'If they won, obviously they care about wrestling.' That was the first thing."

After Price talked to Miller, Miller invited Gardner to visit the campus.

"He said, 'I don't care what you did or didn't do in high school. I want you to come here and compete for a national championship your sophomore year,'" Gardner recalled. "As soon as those words left his face, I was like, 'This is where I'm coming.' That's all I needed to hear. I believed in him from that time."

The plan was to get physically and mentally prepared as a freshman, then seek the gold beginning as a sophomore. Gardner became Wartburg's first heavyweight national champion as a senior, but not before he had a hunch that Miller wasn't fond of him.

"I thought as a freshman that Milboy didn't like me, just because Milboy is kind of stoic and quiet and never talked," Gardner said. "It didn't matter. Somebody had to keep me out of the room, lock the doors. I was going to keep on showing up. I think because he was so sparse with his words that when he did talk to you, it meant a lot. I think Milboy did a good job with, 'You want to matter in this room? Make yourself matter.' You could be the guy in the shadow if you want, hang in the corner, go with all of the lesser opponents you can in practice, but you just won't matter. In that environment, the worst thing that could happen was that you became irrelevant."

Gardner is now head coach of University of the Ozarks in Clarksville, Arkansas.

Miller became immersed in the success of all his wrestlers. Among the Knights he coached was Nick Mitchell, who led Grand View University in Des Moines to its eighth consecutive NAIA national championship in the 2018–19 season.

"He's a great communicator, people know that. He's a great speaker, but he's really good individually too," Mitchell said. "He's good at just keeping things simple. There's not a lot of gray area. He keeps it simple; you know what's expected and he gets a lot out of everybody. He'll turn guys who weren't state champs and weren't the best wrestlers in high school into champs, but he'll get the best out of the best guys too. He gets them to think differently about what they can accomplish; he gets them to think differently about what real work is."

The wrestlers took his words about academics to heart, just as they followed his plan for success on the mat.

"It's hard, obviously, you don't have the scholarship scenario, but you do the best you can and there are ways to get that done," Miller said. "Everything else kind of offset that. The level of kids…I was there twenty-two years and only one student-athlete hasn't graduated. That was important to me too. Wartburg's a place where they celebrate success in everything—celebrate academics, celebrate music, celebrate athletics. I like that."

The campus liked Miller, too. If there was an enticing offer from a bigger school, Wartburg's administration did what it could to get him to stay. So did the boosters and the students.

"Wartburg didn't back down when a D-1 thing came. We talked about those kind of things in the administration at the time. They stepped up some," Miller said. "I mean just the point that they wanted you to stay was a big factor. Not just the administration but the community, the boosters, the kids, the alums. There was one time during that span that I thought I was going to leave, and that did happen. That was a hard pull for us. We actually stopped and re-thought the whole process and ended up *not* leaving."

Miller made a name for the program's success with the motto "Do It Anyway." There are other Milboyisms such as "hold the rope" and "who made that rule?" or "change the tape."

"He never believed in saying 'No.' 'You can't do that,' 'You shouldn't be able to do that.' He never believed in saying no as in 'Why can't we?'" Breitbach said. "He believed strongly in his 'Do it anyway' philosophy. You don't have to have a reason, like a kid saying, 'Why daddy, why do I have to do it?' Don't ask questions, just do it anyway."

He also believed strongly in each guy having his own way of doing things, Gardner said.

"The fact that he cared so much about all of us, that permeated everything he did. That's what drove him to find each guy's button, because he cared so much," Gardner said. "The best coaches are able to do that. He did it in a way that still let us be individuals. There are a lot of programs that are successful with a system. With Milboy, there's no system. It changed every year based on every team, based on the guys on that team and what they needed."

Keith Massey, a highly successful coach at Lewis Central High School in Council Bluffs, wrestled at UNI when Miller was an assistant there. He also knew Miller from the freestyle and Greco-Roman circuit in the spring and summer as well as when they became head coaches.

"Milboy, motivationally speaking—I truly believe he lies to every one of his athletes, in a positive way, challenging them," Massey said in the book *Reach for the Stars: The Iowa High School State Wrestling Tournament*. "I kind of stole that from him: 'Prove to me you can do it. I know you can do more. I know you don't think you can, but I know you can,'" Massey said.

The Knights were No. 1 in the Division III rankings by February 1993. They replaced Central on top of the conference tournament then and have not moved from that perch. Wartburg had 37 national champions among 147 all-Americans (finishing among the top eight) during the Miller era; 10 of Miller's champions were one-time state champions in Iowa, and another 9 claimed collegiate gold after having none of it in high school.

"As a coach, probably one of the things I learned the most from him is he takes care of everything," Mitchell said. "I think you hear coaches say sometimes, 'That's not my job' or 'I'm not in the business of this or that.' The way I look at it is because that's not how he was and that's not the way it was when I was at Wartburg and that's not the way it is for us here. Everything is our job. If you want to be good, you have to take care of everything. He doesn't let anything slip through the cracks; it didn't matter the recruiting, the technical side, the personal side, the academic side. If there was an issue, he dealt with it."

After the Knights won two national titles, Miller hired a pair of assistants for the 2000–2001 season. One was Dave Malecek of Osage, and the other was Eric Keller of Indianola. They were all-Americans at Northern Iowa after being two-time state champions in high school. Keller took over as head coach at North Central in Naperville, Illinois, for the 2005–6 season—he was named Division III rookie coach of the year—and Malecek moved to his current position at Wisconsin-LaCrosse beginning with the 2006–7 season.

Keller's arrival at Wartburg sounds much like Miller's. After competing at UNI, Keller was trying to decide if he wanted to go to Nebraska, where UNI coach Mark Manning had just been hired, or stay with the Panthers, who elevated assistant Brad Penrith to head coach.

"I guess I'm not even sure how this came to be, but Milboy called me and wanted me to just come take a look," Keller said. "Just come take a look at Wartburg. That wasn't even on my radar at the time."

Miller concurred with Keller's comment about the job idea, adding, "We just kind of clicked."

Keller said he'd been to Wartburg for wrestling previously. Early impressions were that it was a special place for the sport. He didn't have a great understanding of Division III then, and he knew Miller from seeing each other at UNI events, but not on a personal level. One visit told Keller they seemed to think alike about moving the sport forward.

So began Keller's three tours of wrestling work under the direction of a man named Jim Miller.

"Those were some really, really fun years," Keller said of his time with Miller and Malecek. "I think that's when we really (began to) separate ourselves in a lot of ways. That first year was hard, and that was the year it was at Young Arena (in Waterloo). It was like, 'What's going on?' It became pretty clear, that's why he brought us in.…Some things needed to change. They won it in '96, they had just won it in '99 and graduated a bunch of people, so it was going to be a rebuilding. That's what it was, a rebuilding, but it was fun. Guys bought in and it paid off because in 2003 and 2004 we won both of those titles."

There would be ten more championships for the Knights after that. When your program gets big and successful, where do you go next?

How about Las Vegas? Miller and the Knights—plus thirteen other teams—wrestled in a ballroom of the Flamingo Hilton during the 2004–5 season. The tournament, known as the "Desert Duals," had its sixteenth run in 2018 and has become popular for two key reasons: Las Vegas is usually warmer than Iowa in winter, and the wrestlers get to hit a buffet with no dining limitations after they're done competing.

Keller had an opportunity to miss the Vegas trip. Ohio University coach Joel Greenlee, who was a state champion at Waverly–Shell Rock and an all-American at UNI, had contacted Keller about coming to Ohio. Keller chose to go part of the way east and take a head coaching job for the 2005–6 season at Division III North Central College in Naperville, Illinois.

"I had kind of bought into the Division III philosophy and liked it. The North Central thing, when it came about, you had Naperville, a beautiful place. The AD was the old coach (Jim Miller), so I thought there was going to be some support," Keller said. "That area is a wrestling hotbed, Chicagoland, I saw a lot of positives in it. Leaving Wartburg was really hard."

The Cardinals were 7-0 in duals—only the second undefeated record in program history—under Keller. Squad numbers were thin, but results were good and there were three all-Americans. "As hard as it was to leave Wartburg, it was really, really hard to leave North Central after that first year," Keller said.

But Jim Miller called. Wartburg's Miller, that is.

"That spring I'm going 100 miles per hour recruiting and full-speed ahead, and Milboy calls me," Keller said. "He goes, 'Are you sitting down?' I go, 'I can.' He goes, 'I want you to come back.'"

Keller asked why. Miller said he was getting out, and he wanted Keller to take over the program. Keller became associate head coach and later was named co-head coach of the Knights. Miller's wanting him to take over was strong stuff, Keller said.

"It was pretty humbling. This place, this job, this program, it's unique," Keller said. "It's not like any other place I've been and there are a lot of people that I think would have loved to at least have entertained the idea of it, so for him to have that level of trust, level of belief in me, it was pretty powerful.

"I think one of the main reasons why he called me back was because he did know what my goals were, he did know what my work ethic was, he did know who I am and what I stood for. As the transition happened, everything had already been in place and we'd been through it all to know how it was going to respond to every situation."

Then came the news after the 2012–13 season that Miller was stepping down. Even longtime Wartburg folks such as Breitbach were surprised.

"I'll never forget that day. After the season's over, he and Bobby (Miller's older brother) came over to my house one afternoon, and we were just talking about the future and everything," Breitbach said. "He says, 'I'm going to retire.' I mean it was jaw-dropping, believe me. How do you go from riding the pinnacle here and everything's lined up to continue and (he said), 'I'm retiring.'"

Maybe the time Miller gave to the program and its participants got to be exhaustive.

"He didn't mind the recruiting, he didn't mind the competition, he didn't mind the psychological work that he did," Breitbach said. "That's probably the thing he did the best; getting inside kids' heads and making them believe they were better than they really were. That he didn't mind, but he just said, 'I don't have the fire to go in there and do the technique.'"

A frequent line in hiring processes for athletics jobs is the wish to replace the man who replaced *the man*. Keller was replacing *the man*. There were likely contemporaries awaiting one of Division III's Titanics to hit an iceberg.

"I never viewed it as pressure," Keller said. "It was a level of expectation, and my expectation is excellence for this program. Nobody has a higher expectation of excellence than myself."

He also had his father, Rich Keller, who brought his young son to every Indianola wrestling meet even though the boy's primary goal was to eat as much popcorn as possible. Rich gave his son opportunities to be good in the sport by going to numerous youth tournaments. Rich saw his son win two state championships, the second clinching a team title for Indianola.

"I feel really fortunate to have someone who was always there to build me up," Eric said. "When I needed to have truth, the truth came but it was never in a way of hurtfulness. I feel lucky to have him."

Keller said he has no problem leaving his ego in the car while he goes inside to teach at practice or to coach another meet or tournament.

"For me personally, it will never, ever be about me. Us winning the championship, I love it. It's one of the ultimate things. I want every guy who comes through our program to experience it," Keller said, "but what it really means is a whole bunch of guys got their dream and that changes them forever. It's not a feather in my cap, I want it to be about these guys, changing the way they think and who they become. There are so many egos in this sport, and all an ego in this sport does is interfere with what's important. Level of confidence and self-belief is important because you've got to have that in this sport, because it's such a mental sport, but when it becomes an ego, especially in coaching, all it's going to do is get in the way and interfere with what's important."

To Keller, just like Miller, what's important is getting an individual's hand raised on the final Saturday night of the season.

"It's hard to put into words the high of that feeling," Keller said. "Here's what is so special about it. You've been there every step of the way with them: in that room, in the locker room when they didn't believe they could, when their girlfriend broke up with them or when they were having trouble in a class, dad was being a (pain)....Every story is so different, but ultimately you know all of those struggles, all of those painstaking adversities that they've been through, so when you see them win a national title, it's more than just winning a wrestling match. It's more than just winning a tournament. It's overcoming so many obstacles. You're going to be a source of inspiration for me on days when I come in and I can think about your story and what you did to raise my level of energy, my level of thinking. I'm going to draw inspiration from you off that wall."

Miller was asked what he was most proud of in a Wartburg career that had so many "wow" moments.

"I think the biggest thing was building a program, not just a team. You're including the alums, you're including the boosters, you're including the administration, getting everybody on the same page from the maintenance people to the secretaries to the community...everybody on the same page pulling for the team," Miller answered. "Obviously, the championships were a big deal. Winning the first one in the history of the college, winning the first one in the Iowa Conference. The Iowa Conference schools hadn't won one, the college hadn't won one in anything, all that stuff. We're breaking down barriers as we went and now we get to the point where we own almost every NCAA record in Division III and kept getting higher and higher, we're breaking our own records. That was pretty gratifying. All that stuff was gratifying looking back and it was almost like the reality was bigger than the dream. That doesn't happen in very many people's careers, like actually what happened was way bigger than the dream. I was hoping to win one national title sometimes, you know?

"You're always proud that things that you started didn't fall apart. Obviously, you're proud of here we go, it's still rolling," Miller continued. "I think that's a big part of whether it's a company or whatever, if you can leave and see there is success....I've talked to coaches (who say), 'Man, I don't think I can leave practice even because I think it will fall apart.' I never felt that way."

What if a school wanted to get things going or, God forbid, if a tragedy meant a program needed an experienced hand to take over in an interim basis? Would Miller answer such a call?

"Energy-wise and stuff, I'm not the same, but my passion is there to help people," he said. "I'm looking at what's going on here, I'm looking at what's happening at Grand View with Nick Mitchell and Paul Reedy, both guys who came through my program, and at Loras. You're really gratified to see young people right now still feeling the effect of learning from others and what's going on.

I'm an Iowa guy, a state of Iowa guy. I want to see the state of Iowa dominate Division I, Division II, Division III, NAIA and junior college. We got a trophy in every division (in the 2017–18 season). I'm also looking to help all of the people that have come through my program with the high school programs and so forth. I think I'm just proud that I've been a part of it."

Keller has continued a piece of coaching psychology that Miller got going in the Knights' program and former Wartburg wrestlers such as Gardner took to heart when they took to the mat.

"With Milboy, you believed that when you put that singlet on, you're a superhero, you should win," Gardner said. "If you didn't dominate, let alone win, you felt as if you didn't hold the rope that day."

7
GRAND VIEW

Nick Mitchell knew the definition of the word *irresistible* in 2008 when he applied to be head coach of a new wrestling program at Grand View University in Des Moines.

Those involved in the hiring process found Mitchell to be synonymous with the word.

"He wouldn't let me not hire him. He was recruiting me. If he can do that good of a job recruiting me, he'll be successful recruiting student-athletes," Grand View athletic director Troy Plummer said. "It was a gut feel on Nick. This is the guy I want. If I'm going down in flames, I'm going with that cat because I know it's not going to be from a lack of effort."

The heat of struggle has avoided Plummer and Mitchell throughout the life of the program, which began in the 2008–9 season. Grand View won its eighth consecutive NAIA team championship in the 2018–19 season, becoming a fitting example of the proper use of an uber-abused word—dynasty. The Vikings averaged a gap of 81 points between themselves and second place during the championship eight pack. They have cracked the 200-point barrier three of the last four tournaments, including a record 234.5 points in 2017.

"I love Grand View and what Coach Mitchell does, and how he changes those guys' lives," said Eric Thompson, Grand View's first three-time NAIA champion. "If I was going to send my kid to a college, there's a short list and Grand View's at the top of it."

Grand View lost its first dual meet 22–17 to Wisconsin-Oshkosh on November 14, 2008, but has never lost at home. Since the first national

Nick Mitchell (*back left*) has pointed the way for Grand View University to win eight consecutive NAIA team championships. He started the program and can match the record of Dan Gable's nine straight titles in the 2020 tournament. *Photo by Dan McCool.*

championship came in 2012, Grand View has lost only one meet—a 22–18 decision against NCAA Division I Iowa State on November 7, 2013. On that same day, Grand View beat Division I Drexel University 22–20.

Mitchell said success in his program is built on honesty as well as on hard work.

"If you want stuff to get done, the best approach is always just brutal honesty," Mitchell commented. "You can't get anybody to do anything; they have to trust you. If you want guys to run through a wall for you, you got to trust me that if I ask you to do that, it's what is best for you. You can't build trust if you're fake, or else people are going to see through it over time. It really is about genuinely wanting what's best for the people, not just my athletes but the guys I coach with, my ex-athletes and guys that have coached in the past, and letting those guys know they can trust you. The rest is easy."

Wrestling is arguably the state's best-known sport, and football is popular in the eleven- and eight-man size throughout the state. It was not easy to have a college invest money into starting an athletic program at the time Grand View started a football program and then a wrestling program. Budgets were tight, and extra money was likely put toward building a financial reserve. Grand View, long a sleepy campus on the northeast side of Des Moines with a U.S. highway running through the campus, was making a move with President Kent Henning's approval.

"And that's probably the difference. He had the guts to take a risk," Plummer said.

The initial hope was to run a program the right way and good things may present themselves, Plummer said. That was a similar approach to hiring a football coach when the Vikings named Waterloo native Mike Woodley their first gridiron boss. Woodley, who resigned from Grand View after the 2019 season, was well known throughout high schools and colleges in Iowa, and his hiring—as well as the decision to start football—was front-page news and a highlight story on the evening news. Mitchell graduated from nearby Johnston High School and got to know the state's coaches through his time coaching at NCAA Division III Wartburg College in Waverly. His hiring at Grand View was praised by those who grew potential college grapplers in the state.

"It never entered our minds…a dynasty, national championships, stuff like that," Plummer said. "It was hire good people, do it the right way, be patient and hopefully it will turn out good and start a culture that way."

Mitchell had a rather enviable position as a young coach. If a head coaching position did not appeal to him, Mitchell could stay at Wartburg working in admissions and assisting Jim Miller on the coaching staff of one of the better NCAA Division III teams.

"I didn't really go after a lot of jobs. There were a couple of things I looked at but never was serious about," Mitchell said. "It's interesting because right now, with the growth of college wrestling at the Division II, Division III and NAIA levels, there are so many more jobs opening up. It really wasn't like that when I was coaching (at Wartburg). When there were jobs that opened up, I don't know if I was just lucky or smart, but I just knew I was in a really good situation with Coach Miller, and so I didn't feel like I had to rush on to the next thing.

"So, when this opened up, being that it was in Des Moines, that did really pique my interest. The other thing that really piqued my interest was Coach (Mike) Woodley because he and Coach Miller were good friends. That's how I first heard about it. I knew of his background, I knew he was a really good coach and so I figured a guy like that's going to take a job at a new program here at Grand View, it's got to be a pretty good situation. He had already kind of told Coach Miller of why he thought this could be a great place, so before I even had set foot on campus I was more excited about it because I'd heard some good things from somebody else who was already here. That was a big part of it, just hearing his testimony on what he thought could happen here."

Had he said, "Thanks, but no thanks" to Grand View, Mitchell said he could have become a full-time higher education guy. Maybe director of admissions or in an alumni office.

Woodley and Mitchell engineered the growth on campus, Plummer said.

"Not only did bringing football and wrestling on help our enrollment, it helped us with our culture around here with (Woodley and Mitchell) saying, 'Why not us? We don't have to be OK with just being average,'" Plummer asserted.

Should the Viking wrestlers continue their run in the 2019–20 season, Mitchell will tie legendary Iowa coach Dan Gable for the longest collegiate string of championships. Gable won his nine between 1978 and 1986. The 2019 championship put Mitchell alone in second place, breaking a tie with Vaughan Hitchcock of Cal Poly, who won seven NCAA Division II titles between 1968 and 1974.

Grand View is tied with Adams State of Colorado and Central State of Oklahoma for the most team championships by an NAIA program.

The Vikings gained some national attention during the 2018–19 season by placing fifth at the Reno Tournament of Champions. The top four were all NCAA Division I programs: Oklahoma State, Michigan State, Old Dominion and Wyoming.

It was also announced during the season that Grand View would start a women's wrestling program in the 2019–20 season. Angelo Crinzi, a former Grand View wrestler, was hired to bring the program to life.

Mitchell came to Grand View after being an all-American wrestler and an assistant coach at Wartburg. His mentor is Jim Miller, who led the Knights to ten team championships. Miller left a voice message on Plummer's phone suggesting the Vikings look at Mitchell as coach.

"I'm like, 'I'm no brain surgeon, but I know who Jim Miller is and what he's done. If that guy is calling to put his stamp on a guy, I need to have a conversation with him,'" Plummer said. "At that point, Nick wasn't in the mix. He was just a guy who turned in a résumé. I heard (Miller's message), and I was like, 'I wanna take a longer look.' I talked to Coach Woodley. Woodley called Miller and got some more background and said, 'This guy's got it.'

"Then I took a deeper dive into it and saw that he had an admissions background. He was a coach for a number of years, and he understood the financial aid process, understood all of small college athletics and was ready to take over a program," Plummer added. "Brought him in for an official interview and it went great. He was exactly what I thought I was looking for."

Plummer was early in his tenure as athletic director when Grand View decided to start a wrestling program. He felt Mitchell was his man early on, but the quality credentials of other applicants necessitated more interviews. After a second interview with Mitchell, Plummer said Mitchell was the right fit for what he wanted to do.

Miller echoed Plummer's assessment of his candidate: "I think (Mitchell) was a no-brainer. I knew he could coach; I knew he could inspire kids. He had already been in admissions and dealt with financial aid and he knew recruiting. He's from Johnston, Iowa. I don't know how many more check marks you could check off. I knew his passion of helping kids and building a program."

Miller was asked if he was surprised at Mitchell's success as a coach. The Vikings have never finished out of the top ten in the NAIA tournament.

"Not surprised, but I am surprised maybe in the dominance that it's happened in," Miller said of Mitchell's success. "Not just winning, just dominating the whole division in that respect. They're running circles around everybody."

Apparently, Mitchell and associate head coach Paul Reedy are working circles around everyone else. Except for a few hours of fun at the after party, those two are immersed in recruiting new talent, sharpening the current squad and making sure everything gets done right. Mitchell likes to call it living a championship lifestyle, and it's become a mantra of oversized success in and out of the oversized practice room that used to be part of a bowling alley.

"(Mitchell) goes above and beyond what he needs to do. I think a lot of coaches don't realize in order to be the best coach and have the best team, you've really got to know each and every one of your wrestlers," Grand View 197-pounder Evan Hansen said. "He has to put in a lot of time with every one of us and figure out what makes us tick. Like if you're a guy that can't be yelled at, he won't yell at you, but he'll figure out another way to get you to do what needs to be done."

Hansen, who won two state high school championships while competing on an Exira/Elk Horn–Kimballton squad that numbered six wrestlers, won his third NAIA championship in 2019. He could become the eighth

Evan Hansen of Grand View University (shooting for a takedown) comes into the 2019–20 season seeking a fourth NAIA national championship. Hansen won two state championships at Exira/Elk Horn–Kimballton High School and could become the eighth four-time champion in NAIA history. *Photo by Dan McCool.*

four-time champion in 2020. Hansen is an example of the "championship lifestyle" success that Mitchell speaks of frequently.

"For me, I decided if I'm going to go to college and spend thousands of dollars to wrestle and get a diploma, I'm going to do the best I can on and off the mat," Hansen said. "So that meant putting everything aside and just focusing. That was a main part of why I came to Grand View, because I knew Mitchell would help me do that."

Hansen also got an assist from Mitchell in planning a life partnership during the 2018–19 season. Hansen is engaged to Rachel Watters, a wrestler at Oklahoma City University who was an Olympic Trials qualifier in women's freestyle wrestling in 2016 while attending Ballard High School at Huxley, Iowa. Mitchell was among the first to know of Hansen's plan to propose.

Eric Thompson was on top of the world as a senior at Waverly–Shell Rock High School in 2008. Thompson was the No. 1 big man recruit nationally, and he selected a scholarship offer from Iowa State University. By the time his college eligibility was finished, Thompson was a three-time national champion—at Grand View.

"When I got to college, it was more so immaturity, just childish stuff," Thompson said. "Sometimes when you go to college it's different and it's a lot easier to kind of lose track of what you're actually showing up there to do."

After a breakup with wrestling, Thompson was working and not necessarily enjoying it. Thompson said he was in the "Poor me. Why didn't it work out for me?" phase that every kid seems to go through. When Mitchell made contact about Thompson getting back on the mat, Thompson listened because of one option school presented to him. Mitchell's recruiting effort included the "championship lifestyle" pitch.

"He sells that on his recruiting trip to me. It was me and my parents, and I was completely lost in life. I didn't know what I wanted," Thompson said. "I knew I didn't want to go back to my job at the Target distribution center. He's telling me all this stuff and he's saying all these things, then he gives me the scholarship papers and I'm like, 'I'm in. I'll sign them right now.' He could have said nothing, and I think I would have been in. Mitchell and Reedy were the perfect guys at the perfect time to kind of tell me to 'quit being a wuss about it, you've got to get back to work, go to school and get better at wrestling.' That's kind of what I needed."

Why, after he and wrestling had such acrimony?

"I didn't want to work anymore. I didn't want to do that Target distribution center, but at the same time I had a connection with him, and Coach Reedy as well," Thompson said. "The time that Coach Mitchell and Coach Reedy put into my life and how I was living and the psychology of everything I was feeling at the time, they definitely broke me down and built me back up to who I am now."

Thompson was named NAIA "Wrestler of the Year" after collecting a pin in the national finals in 2012, then scored a pin in the 2013 tournament that clinched Grand View's second team title in a row. He added a victory by technical fall as a senior in 2014, becoming the young program's first three-time champion.

That kind of celebrating, including a sweat-soaked Thompson hugging Plummer after a championship effort, was what Mitchell had planned for the Vikings at the beginning.

President Henning remembered first getting the idea Mitchell would find a way to make that plan happen after the Vikings tied for ninth place in the 2010 tournament at Oklahoma City. Glenn Rhees won the 174-pound championship—he was the program's second individual titlist—but Henning said Mitchell had a better team finish in mind. At tournament's end, the team and individual awards were being presented and teams were gathering their gear to leave.

"I was congratulating the team; they were kind of rounding themselves up. Nick was not happy," Henning remembered. "As they were leaving the (arena), Nick turned around, he looked up at the stage with just that look. What I saw was just the determination…I even said to him, 'You'll be there someday.' It was just the look on his face. His last look before leaving was to look back up on that stage and they were awarding this trophy. It was the determination. I could see that he had his sights set on having his team there, claiming that national championship. It was just that gut feel that that's what I was looking at. I was looking at this coach saying, 'I'm going to be there.' He never doubted that he could get to a championship stage."

Two years later, Mitchell and the Vikings were on that stage—it happened to be in Des Moines—accepting the team championship trophy. They finished 31 points ahead of Southern Oregon. Mitchell's two daughters, Brynn and Paige, have an annual photo with the championship trophy because they've never known what the runner-up prize looks like.

Their dad wants to see how good the Vikings can be.

"I want to see what the real potential is of our team and our program. That really drives me just to find out how good we can be," Mitchell said.

Henning remembered a similar approach to winning big when interviewing Woodley for the football job. Woodley coached at the high school, small college and Division I level in Iowa. He was coaching and in administration in Texas when Plummer used long ties to the family to get him interested in the Grand View job.

"He said, 'I think at this point to cap off my career, coming back to Iowa and starting a program, building it from scratch and then taking it to a national championship, that would be a wonderful way for me to finish out my career,'" Henning said. "When he said it, I thought, 'Nice answer for an interview. Will I ever see it?' That was 2007, and you know what happened in 2013. I saw it.

"I reminded him of that conversation on the field (in Rome, Georgia) when we were celebrating the championship," Henning said.

Woodley resigned as football coach after the 2018 season. His son, Joe, took over the head coach position.

Mitchell had learned the championship mentality during his time at Wartburg. He brought it to Grand View and didn't hoard the champagne when the success started. The coach he and nearly everyone else call

"Milboy" was working on the next success as soon as the after party died down. There is time to reflect on success later, Mitchell said.

"Every single year at the national tournament, I'm still thinking ahead to the next year. There's hardly any time where you sit back and really feel good about things," Mitchell said. "We tell our guys every year, 'If you win the title at the end, you can feel good about it, but you can feel good and work at the same time. You don't have to stop working to pat yourself on the back.'"

Success helped squad numbers grow to the point that the practice room was too small. The team was having split practices, but Mitchell said the "If you build it, they will come" philosophy does not work in small college athletics. And hearing "No" from the administration is a reason to think outside the box rather than stew about what might have been.

"We got our roster up to where we couldn't afford to be in this room anymore," Mitchell said. "It was going to be a liability. Then on top of that, when we built the new facility, it wasn't just Grand View dollars. We fundraised a lot of money, about $250,000 of our own money, to help pay for that. So when you hear a 'No,' it's more about, 'What do we have to do to get a 'Yes'?'"

Count Mitchell among those who *love* what they do. "I like being here, I like being with the team. None of that feels like sacrifice to me. Even some of the stuff that maybe a lot of coaches don't like doing, I don't mind it. I like all parts of this job. It's a lot easier to put a lot of time into it when it's something that you love to do."

The Mitchell system, the "championship lifestyle," requires a student-athlete love to wrestle yet be willing to pursue excellence in the classroom as well. His attention to doing little things well might stem from time spent with his youth wrestling club coach, Rick Lewis, a longtime assistant at Des Moines Lincoln, and from his high school coach, Frank Baltzley.

"Starting out in my kids club with coach Rick Lewis, I just remember they were really good at teaching the basics there. It wasn't the type of club where you were going to learn a bunch of headlocks and throws, garbage-type stuff," Mitchell said. "I've always been a big believer in basics first, winning by being great at the little things. Coach Lewis was clearly a spiritual guy; his faith has always really directed him, and that's the same with me. So, seeing that, somebody who modeled that at an early age, made a difference for me. With Coach Baltzley, he just had such a good connection with the guys on the team. People loved him so much, they loved wrestling for him."

Miller and his methods also had a profound impact on Mitchell.

"Aside from my parents, he's probably had as much or more influence than anybody on my life," Mitchell said. "When I was young and first in college, he was a guy to keep my head on straight and keep me focused. But probably the biggest thing as a mentor over the last ten years is helping me raise the bar on what I thought we could accomplish here. Honestly, when I got to Grand View, I wanted to win a national title as a team, but it was an expectation. That was what I was part of for the past twelve years at Wartburg as an athlete and as a coach, so when I got here I just decided there wasn't going to be anything different. Why should we not win?

"That's just being around him for that amount of time. That's the way he thinks, that's how he is and so it just rubbed off," Mitchell added. "There's a big difference between a goal and an expectation. That's what it was, just an expectation. Nothing else is going to be acceptable other than that. That's the way it's been."

Mitchell's ability to motivate has grown beyond the practice room. Occasionally, his words can be heard in Henning's office. Henning said Mitchell's championship lifestyle approach has permeated the campus.

"It is so powerful there have been times when I kind of need a little pick-me-up and I call up the YouTube and I listen to a little bit of Nick Mitchell on what are you going to sacrifice for your goals," Henning said. "What are you going to do? Life isn't easy, people are going to knock you down. What are you going to do to get up?"

Mitchell had experience in being knocked down short of a goal, which he said helps him in relating to a Grand View wrestler going through a similar experience.

"I was a better college wrestler because I didn't win a state title. I had some really tough competition during those years in high school and the same thing in college. I came up short of what I wanted," Mitchell said. "As a coach, I think I'm better because I've been pretty good at looking back at my career and being honest with myself about why I came up short and what those areas were: whether it was the mental aspect, my training or academically maybe not buying into that championship lifestyle when I was in school. I think the more honest I can be with myself about those things, the easier it is for me to pass that on to my guys because I know what they're thinking. I've been there and I understand there's a reason why you don't get what you want."

He's had sixteen men win a total of twenty-eight national championships, beginning with Matt Burns of Urbandale in 2009, but there have been fifteen runner-up finishes by fourteen of Mitchell's wrestlers. An unsatisfactory

Saturday night hasn't changed through the years, Mitchell said. He was second in the 1999 NCAA Division III tournament.

"It's a flashback is what it is," Mitchell said. "You're nineteen again and coming up short of your goal and it hurts, and it sucks. You see that in those kids, and you know exactly what they're feeling. It's real similar."

Thompson said he saw Mitchell's care about individual success up close when his roommate at the time, Brad Lower, finished second in the national tournament.

"I was upset, but I don't think Mitchell could hardly sleep after that," Thompson said. "That's all he could think about, and that was a microcosm for how much he cares about people, how much he cares about the kids who don't win, the kids who don't get what they want."

Thompson, who's been out of Grand View five years as of this writing, said he's frequently on the phone with Mitchell and with Reedy. "I see myself talking to them like that the rest of my life," Thompson said.

Such love of program and personnel was plentiful when Grand View held a ten-year reunion for the program in 2018. Thompson said this was not like a high school class reunion.

"This was different, it was people you couldn't wait to see," Thompson said. "All you could feel in that room was love. Everyone was so excited to see people they hadn't seen (for a while)."

Mitchell wanted to avoid having one particular reunion after he got the Grand View job. That's with Reedy, who Mitchell was able to keep from taking a high school coaching job in New Orleans. Mitchell and some mutual friends even had a going-away party for Reedy, who was known to come to practice when he was an assistant coach at nearby Perry High School and there was a snow day. Mitchell was assisting at Wartburg when Reedy came to Waverly from Emmetsburg High School.

"Over his time there, I was around him a lot. Actually, we were roommates for a while before I left Waverly," Mitchell said. "The number one thing why we work well together is he thinks like me as far as he's all about the athlete first. Whatever it takes to help those guys accomplish their goals. There's no ego with him. He'll wash mats, he'll do laundry. I walked in the room (one day) to do a technique session, and he's on his hands and knees scrubbing the tape marks off the mat. Because of that, our guys work harder because they see his work ethic, they see how much he cares for them."

When Henning gave the OK to start wrestling at Grand View, Iowa's capital city had not had collegiate wrestling since Drake University discontinued its NCAA Division I program after the 1992–93 season. Henning had restored some athletic programs that had been discontinued because of financial straits, and he'd approved the start of a football program as well. Nine months after the wrestling team won Grand View's first national championship, the football team won the NAIA title. There has been more than just a new trophy to display when a new sport came online, Henning said.

"Every time we have started a sport, it has contributed positively to the institution's bottom line Year One," Henning said. "On an ongoing operational expense basis, what people have to remember is the revenue is the tuition and room and board that our students are bringing to campus. If they're not enrolled here, we get zero. Yes, we offer athletic scholarships, but not all of our athletes are getting full rides. As a matter of fact, relatively few would be on a full-tuition scholarship. If they are, that's a combination of their academic award and their athletic award. They're getting a scholarship, but they're still paying some portion of our tuition. And if they're living on campus, they're paying room and board."

Henning said hiring Plummer to direct the athletic department has been a big positive. The Vikings have won a total of twelve national championships—football, men's volleyball, men's golf and shooting sports joining the eight wrestling trophies—under Plummer's direction.

Plummer remembered interviewing with Henning about the athletic director position. In one statement, he learned plenty about his future boss: "As he was about to green-light me, he said, 'I'll tell you one thing: I want a guy that I have to pull the reins back on, not someone I have to whip to get going,'" Plummer recalled. "That said to me not just with athletics but with everything, 'Let's go, let's push forward and push the envelope, not just sit with what the status quo is and how everybody else thinks this is supposed to be. Let's kind of forge our own path a little bit.' He's always been extremely supportive as long as you can show him that it makes sense."

In many cases, a highly successful young coach and a small college or university aren't long for each other. Mitchell held the championship trophy for the eighth time one month shy of his forty-first birthday. He said celebrating many more birthdays at Grand View wasn't out of the question.

"There's Division I jobs where you're realistically never going to win. I don't see myself being happy with something like that," Mitchell said. "I want to be in a situation where I feel like I have a legitimate chance to be successful. I love where I'm at and who the people are that I'm with every day. You can't get wrapped up in some of the maybe surface-type stuff that really isn't that important in the long run."

There have been inquiries about Mitchell, Henning said.

High school and college wrestling tournaments are popular in Iowa and a sure sign that the season is getting into full swing. Here, fans ring the balcony as well as sit in bleachers at Southeast Polk High School in suburban Des Moines to watch matches on the ten mats in the Grand View Open. *Photo by Dan McCool.*

"You can hardly fault somebody for wanting to reach further, particularly somebody who's driven like that," Henning admitted, "and then if that happens, it's easier to fill the vacancy with somebody really good because they see us as an opportunity to do the same thing. You can be sure that his phone started to ring after his first national championship. My phone has rung over the years with opportunities to go to different institutions."

But Henning also points to Miller and how his long stay at Wartburg may have impacted Mitchell's making career plans.

"Nick had a very important model and mentor who lived that—know your place in life," Henning said. "His mentor had those opportunities and passed them up, and realized his place was at Wartburg."

Mitchell agreed. "Coach Miller had a great career at Wartburg, had a couple of opportunities to move on if he wanted to, but he's a pretty good example of just being at a place where if you can have all of the pieces that are most important—at least what I consider most important—then there is no reason to move on."

Thompson said Mitchell was an excellent mentor to him.

"He's a special person. I think my wife (Sarah) has said thank you to Coach Mitchell before, and to Coach Reedy. You could ask almost every guy that's come through the program....We all got better at wrestling, and obviously the success is there, but forever my life has changed for the better since I went to Grand View and I was around those two," Thompson said. "If you have the right mindset and the right attributes and all of these things in your life, you're going to end up where you're supposed to. I made wrong choices when I was at Iowa State, lots of them, can't number them, and it led me to Grand View. I think that's where I was supposed to be, to be honest. They were the people I was supposed to be around. I think they were the people I needed. I think it was the right place at the right time for me. I needed that kind of help that they were able to provide."

Henning could provide the wrestling office some knowledge of wrestling. He graduated from Wartburg, so Henning knew of what Miller and the Knights had done. Henning graduated from MFL High School in Monona, and his nephew Travis Henning was a state champion wrestler for the Bulldogs. He knew wrestling was a big deal in Iowa.

Henning also knew teams can wear out their welcome with a long stay at the top. He worked at Duke University when it went back-to-back in NCAA basketball. "We learn to play 'King of the Mountain' when we're kids," Henning said. "You try to get to the top of the mountain, and as soon as somebody's there, you try to knock them off."

Plummer said anyone wanting to bump Mitchell off the mountain has work to do before the ascension to the top. "You know how Nick Mitchell is better than everybody else? It's because he out-works everybody else, and it's really that simple."

8
JUNIOR COLLEGE

Kaye Young was a Renaissance man whose life experiences included being a published author of poetry, an actor in community theater, a student of fire-eating in the circus and a wandering soul who experienced migrant work and the hop-a-train life of a hobo.

Young was also a wrestling coach who experienced individual and team success. Newspaper accounts of his hiring reported Young was paid $1,200 for his first season at North Iowa Area Community College in Mason City. That was on top of his salary as a counselor at the school. His team won the national junior college championship in 1973. Three individuals were national champions during his watch, including two-time king Joe Hatchett of Cedar Rapids, Washington. Prior to starting that program, Young led Ron Rice of NU High of Cedar Falls to a state title in 1959, coached Maquoketa to a 76-16 record in seven years and spent one season at Wartburg College.

NIACC was the first Iowa program to win a junior college team championship. Iowa Central Community College in Fort Dodge won the second title in 1981, and the Tritons added seven more between 2002 and 2017. There have been twenty-six Iowa high school graduates who were junior college national champions through the 2019 meet, beginning with Floyd Shade of Des Moines Tech at Lamar Junior College of Colorado in 1965. Hatchett was the first two-time champion; Tyler Hoffman of East Buchanan and ICCC joined him in 2015 and 2016.

Hatchett, a multitalented athlete, said Young was a coach who found creative ways to make his athletes better or able to adjust to situations an

Distance does not separate brothers when it comes to supporting a wrestler's effort. Prior to the 2019 NAIA tournament, Justin Portillo of Grand View University warmed up with his twin brother, Josh, who wrestled at NCAA Division II Nebraska-Kearney. The Portillo twins, who combined for five state championships at Clarion High School, each earned all-America honors in 2019. *Photo by Dan McCool.*

opponent caused. Hatchett was privy to one of those distinctive drills, as were a few other NIACC student-athletes. It was after Hatchett won his first national championship in 1970 and was working on a repeat performance. Young thought it would be good for Hatchett to experience the frustration of facing lanky, long-armed opponents who could keep him outside or the opponents who would charge in and try to reduce his strength.

"They were coming. He had football players; he even had some basketball players come up there to wrestle me. The basketball players are tall, and they could kind of keep me away. I couldn't use my strength on them, but they could put the hands down and I had to work my way in there," Hatchett said. "A lot of football players, after practice, I'd be on the mat with them for about a half-hour, forty-five minutes and I'd be in that circle and they would come at me.

The community colleges in Iowa have a habit of being a major player in the national junior college tournament. Two of the coaches are Cole Spree of Ellsworth College of Iowa Falls (*left*) and Cody Alesch of Iowa Lakes Community College in Estherville, shown comparing post-meet notes. *Photo by Dan McCool.*

"I could take anybody down who I wanted to take down, but he kept sending them to me. Some of them really didn't know how to wrestle, but the idea was he wanted to get me tired, so I had to work. And then he would let them put a figure-four on me or put their legs in on me and I would have to work my way out."

Hatchett finished his career at NIACC with a 39-0 record and a trophy for being voted outstanding wrestler of the 1971 national tournament. He also has fond memories of his time with Young.

"Coach Young, he and I got along like he was my dad. He'd be showing me stuff, like he showed it on me and put it on so tight my jaw went like that," Hatchett said, making a noise as if his jaw was cracking. "Then I jumped up and I said, 'OK, coach, my turn.' He goes, 'No, I am just showing you.'

"He was also a counselor. If you had a problem with something, you could go to his office or go to his house, sit down and talk to him and he would really listen to you and try to help you out. He was not going to tell you what to do, he'd give you a few things and one of those ways would help you in your situation. That's how Coach was."

Doug Trees of Greene remembered Young as a man who had high expectations of his charges, but he was not the type of coach to harp on something such as a loss that was likely a one-of-those-nights thing. Trees, who was the seventh wrestler in Iowa high school history to wrestle in the state finals all four years, spoke of a quadrangular meet at Muscatine Community College that was highlighted by Trees beating Paul Graham of Muscatine CC. That exacted a bit of revenge for a loss to Graham in the Class A state finals in 1967. But there was a match at Muscatine prior to facing Graham that Trees wanted to forget.

"I just knew that when you stepped up on the mat with Young, he expected things out of you, but yet he wasn't real strict," Trees said. "I remember at that quadrangular we went to, I got beat second round by a kid that I should have never lost to. I was ahead of him, and I wrestled a crappy match and got beat. I came off the mat, and Young was actually smiling and kind of snickered about it. He knew I shouldn't have been beat, but it wasn't a big deal. I learned something from getting beat. That's what he said—next time you'll be ready for him."

Trees said he chose NIACC after taking a recruiting trip to the University of Iowa.

"(Young) kind of looked into me and got hold of me, talked to me a little bit on the phone and stuff, but I never actually went there and looked it over," Trees said. "I went down to the University of Iowa and stayed there for a weekend. Iowa was looking at me, and I stayed with the wrestlers for a weekend down there. They didn't really offer me much of a scholarship. Back then, it was hard to get a scholarship. I figured rather than go to a four-year school to start with, I'd start with a junior college, so I picked NIACC to go to."

Young had a future Olympian start his postsecondary wrestling career at NIACC. That was Joe Corso, a state champion from West Des Moines Valley, who competed on the 1976 Olympics freestyle team. Corso, who was adopted from Italy as a young boy, later was an all-American at Purdue before he made the Olympics. The time in Mason City was valuable, even if the rewards were less than what Corso wanted.

"I took fifth in the junior college nationals two years in a row. Do you think I felt lower than a snake in a wagon rut? Absolutely, but I didn't let it bother me," Corso said. "Everything I did was a learning experience. I tried to keep my blinders focused here (in front), but I kept my mind open to learning the technique, learning what I needed to do to get better."

For Hatchett and Trees and their teammates, wrestling season meant going to church every day. There was no need to pray because the Trojans were regular winners. The church was the site of practice for NIACC's team. The campus that presently sits on the east side of Mason City was not yet built, so the wrestling team worked out in a church, but only after the women's sewing group was done.

"That church that we wrestled in, they'd roll the mats up and they'd have sewing classes in there for older ladies. We'd have to take the sewing machines and put them all at one end of the room and roll the mat out so we could wrestle in there," Trees recalled.

Hatchett remembered opponents heard about the practice facilities, and the jabs began. Compared to other sites the Trojans wrestled at, NIACC's facilities were hardly the stuff that drew in good talent. Hatchett liked that.

"That's what people said, 'No wonder you guys win all of the meets you guys are in. You got God on your side.' I said, 'Well, it ain't the devil,'" Hatchett joked. "All the rest of the colleges we went to, they had all of the big facilities: clean room, you could turn the heat up if you had to, everything was all padded, they had weight equipment, they had things to help you lose weight. We didn't have any of that; we did it the hard way. If I had to do it again, I'd like to have it the hard way again."

That "hard way" built a thirty-seven-meet winning streak at NIACC. It was halted, 22–14, during a road trip to Colorado on February 5, 1971. The Trojans lost only five duals and had one tie through the 1971–72 season, when NIACC finished second in the NJCAA tournament for the third consecutive time. The Trojans had a bright immediate future because seven freshmen were returning for the 1972–73 season after the team lost the team title that Young so wanted by one half point. The only loss to graduation was national champion Tom Garcia, a Mason City High School product.

The 1973 tournament had Bob Fouts of Waterloo West win the national heavyweight championship, and Dedric Doolin of Cedar Rapids Jefferson and Ed Herman of Johnston each finish second. Bruce Wilson of Waterloo West was fourth, and Joe Corso of West Des Moines Valley placed fifth. Three years later, Corso would compete in freestyle at the 1976 Olympics and the NIACC wrestling program was discontinued.

After the 1973 title, Young said, "This tops it all off. We have gotten stronger each year and now we are on the top. We can't keep climbing from here, but now we have to try to stay on top."

The NIACC program was idle after finishing thirty-third in the 1976 national tournament, then reinstalled for the 2007–8 season. Young stepped down from the head coaching spot after the 1976 meet.

For all the success he had in Mason City, Hatchett said he never got into being cocky about winning his next bout. Not even after he won his first national championship. He wanted to take care of business each time.

"No. I never think that. It doesn't make a difference of who you are," Hatchett said. "Every opponent I wrestled, I didn't care what record they had, I think there's an opportunity to beat me, so that's the way I wrestled. You just don't know."

Hatchett learned a lesson about always being on the offense when he had a match against an opponent who was not supposed to challenge a No. 1 seed like him.

"We shook hands, I went to step back, and he shot in on me, almost took me down. I wasn't expecting it, right? I said to myself, 'Man, Joe, you got to put this guy away,'" Hatchett said. "So when we went back to the middle again, I put a head chancery on him and I threw him, I just locked him up right there. At first he was fighting me, and then all of a sudden he stopped fighting. The ref slapped the mat, I got up and he laid there, was out cold and it took three of those smelling salts things to bring him back around."

Hatchett said he was a good guy, easy to get along with, until someone stood across from him on a wrestling mat. Then it was all about business, and business was always good for Hatchett. That didn't mean he could always keep his cool.

"There were a couple of times we wrestled up in the boonies, and (Young) told me, 'Joe, they don't like blacks' and I was the only black guy on the team. I beat their best guy. It was like a track meet, I was chasing him around the circle, then go around the other way. I finally cornered him off and put the boots to him. Then when I beat him, they threw rotten eggs, rotten tomatoes...whatever. They threw it on the mat at me. Isn't that something? Coach said, 'You guys get Joe,' because I was heading up in the stands. They had to grab me and put me in the locker room."

There were no issues among the NIACC wrestlers, many of whom came from small towns where no black students were enrolled. There was no time to worry about someone's skin tone because it took everything for a varsity guy to keep his spot against some deep talent at his weight. Trees remembered scrapping with Vern Allison for the 118-pound varsity spot.

"I liked NIACC just because we always thought of ourselves as a team as just a bunch of tough nuts," Trees said. "We used to enjoy beating on each other, getting on the mat and doing that to each other. We had a lot of young individuals—Chuck Heene from West Waterloo was there, Vern Allison from Fort Dodge—it was quite an array of people. (Allison) had been through the Marines, and he came back to school. He and I were at the same weight class. He was a hard-nosed little devil, I'll tell you that. We were both trying to make 118 pounds, and I ended up winning that position from him, so he moved up to '26."

Perhaps the only tight time Hatchett had at NIACC was fighting off a takedown attempt by teammate Matt Clarke, who was a state champion from Eldora. "Me and Matt were like brothers," Hatchett said.

"Matt's the kind of person that when he wrestles, he keeps you on the edge of your seat because he wrestles so loose," Hatchett said. "He knows judo, a lot of throws and stuff and he wrestles so loose and everybody's so nervous. Ol' Matt, he was always wanting to take me down. Matt got in on me all the way, he was getting ready to take me down, and I go, 'Oh, oh, oh, my leg' and Coach blows the whistle and goes, 'Matt, let him go, let him go, let him go.'"

Turned out there was no true injury, and Hatchett kept up his tricks on Clarke. The guys on the NIACC roster took care of one another, Hatchett said. "We had a good family there because everybody looked out for each other. Everybody worked together on that team."

Trees said his time at NIACC was some of the best times of his life.

"I'll never forget it. It's been forty-nine years ago, and I still sit here and see everybody's face just like they're sitting here with me. It's something you don't forget," Trees said in a 2019 interview. "I remember each of their styles. One big family, more or less. A wrestling family if you want to call it that. You almost felt like if you lost a match, you let the team down. That wasn't the case, but that's what you felt like when you wrestled for Kaye. He just made you feel like one big family."

It took time for the wrestling family to come together at Iowa Central in Fort Dodge. That had nothing to do with cliques or differences of opinion. When Dennie Friederichs was hired in 1972 to take over for Ron Jones, Iowa Central's wrestling program was in Eagle Grove and the team was known as the Pirates. They were the second and third coach of the program. Richard Griessel was the coach of the first ICCC squad.

Friederichs was a Fort Dodge kid who wrestled for Harold Nichols at Iowa State and earned all-America honors three times. His low-key approach made people wonder if he was right for coaching wrestling, especially at that time, when the top coaches in the area were vociferous and demonstrative.

"Nichols was pretty quiet," Friederichs said of the man who won six NCAA Division I team championships and 492 dual meets at Iowa State.

Nichols had a strong influence on how Friederichs coached.

"Nick was the best coach I ever had, and he was tough on you, but you never heard too much out of him. That was kind of surprising back then," Friederichs said. "Not many people know this, but this is back in 1957, '58, Nick never had very many organized practices. That probably would surprise a lot of people. We would go in and wrestle hard for a couple of hours, just keep going. We got in good shape, but he didn't believe too much in running. We'd run during the Christmas vacation, but other than that he was more interested in just wrestling. He always said that if you had a choice between running and wrestling, he'd rather have you wrestle, that you were improving and getting in shape. We were under the old stadium at Iowa State. We had a big long hallway, but nobody ever thought of sprinting much. Now it's a big part of wrestling, getting your lungs in shape. There was no organized weightlifting. I'd go down to the gymnastics room a lot, do chin-ups and stuff like that. We never actually lifted weights."

Just as Nichols was successful in Ames, Friederichs was pretty successful at Iowa Central. He had a 240-80-2 record in duals and had nine individual national championships in a twenty-four-year career. Al Frost of Nashua found a polar opposite of a coach when he came to ICCC in Fort Dodge. At Nashua, Frost had a wrestling coach named Gerald Bakke who rarely stood still long enough to watch a complete match because he was all over the team's side of the gymnasium. If it was a win, especially an upset, Bakke would display an excellent vertical leap even though his stature was more in line with Danny DeVito's than Dan Gable's.

Al Frost said he was not interested in wrestling after high school. Then he met Iowa Central Community College coach Dennie Friederichs. Frost earned all-America honors for the Tritons, wrestled at Iowa and embarked on his own coaching career, which includes over four hundred victories and a dual-meet state championship. *Photo by Dan McCool.*

Frost had his start in wrestling as a freshman in high school. As a seventh and eighth grader, he played basketball.

"My mom (Shirley) was from a town, Rockwell, Iowa, which did not have wrestling. All she knew about wrestling was what they saw on TV back then, which was (like the WWE), and she said, 'You're not doing that,'" Al said. "In a roundabout way, I said, 'Wrestling is not that, not hitting people over the head with chairs.' But I still had to play basketball by her choice.

"I wasn't bad at it, but I seemed to get a lot of fouls. Gerry Bakke, I'd seen him in the hallway a few times doing what coaches do—kind of recruiting. I kept pestering mom, and she finally gave in, so my freshman year in high school was the first time I ever had any experience in wrestling. That's when I started knowing Gerald Bakke. By the time my second year came around, a lot of us didn't realize it but we had a pretty good crowd, a pretty good following watching Nashua wrestling. We were pretty decent but come to realize a lot of people had said they came just to watch Bakke during the meets. He was all over the place, screaming, yelling, standing on chairs—he was only like 4-foot nothing—sitting on the back of the chair with his feet in the chair. He did a lot of interesting finagling and stuff in the matches. Us as wrestlers, we got used to it, and he was a great PR guy."

Friederichs remembered Frost initially for an interview when the coach was looking for talent and Frost was apparently not fired up about continuing his studies.

"I got quite a few kids who didn't even think of going to school much, you had to talk them into going to school," Friederichs said. "I can always remember Al Frost. I remember him coming in with his mother, and I said, 'What would you like to do, where would you like to be five or six years from now?' He said, 'I don't know.' I said, 'Are you interested in going to school?' (and he was). 'I don't know.' He ended up being one of the nicest kids and went on to Iowa. If it wasn't for injuries, he'd have been a national champ for us. Then he went to Iowa, and he was really tough, but he got injured."

Frost thought a farm power program Iowa Central offered looked pretty good. It was an eleven-month course, so he came to school and went to wrestling practice. He said there were a couple of other schools he looked at, but they did not have the farm program and an end in a year.

"Dennie, he was a great guy, great family, but a whole different character than what Gerald Bakke was," Frost said. "He never yelled that I can *ever* remember. I hardly ever remember seeing him get mad, maybe one time, so you didn't really know how to read him until you got to know him. A lot of us wrestlers at that level that start feeding on each other, got each other going. We were third my freshman year and were national champs my sophomore year. I was blessed with two great coaches to start out my wrestling career. I don't know how to really explain it to you, was it tough to make a transition or not? I don't recall it being tough, but it was just unique. It was different going from one to the other."

As it turned out, Frost did not graduate from the farm power program. After finishing fourth nationally as a freshman, he began to think about coaching the sport he loved. He began classes that leaned more toward education, got his degree, moved to Iowa to wrestle for Dan Gable and recently notched his 400th coaching victory at Nashua-Plainfield High School.

"I guess at that point in time, I still didn't have a clue once I left Iowa Central what direction I was even going to go when I went to Iowa," Frost said. "I don't even know who pointed me in the direction of education other than the fact that I found out I wasn't a bad wrestler; maybe I can coach this sport too. I figured if I want to coach it, then teaching was probably going to be the best fit for that. The rest is history. I got into education courses at Iowa. I had to spend three years there. I ended up redshirting my first year at Iowa and had two years of eligibility after that. I'd lost pretty much any credits that were towards any kind of a bachelor of science degree because that farm power program didn't get me much."

Friederichs said he had over twenty individuals become coaches after their time at Iowa Central was exhausted. He said the thank-yous were special because of the growth some of those individuals made during their time with him. "Their frame of mind when they got out of high school, it wasn't even a dream of theirs. Sometimes you talk a kid into going to school, and he ends up being very successful the rest of his life," Friederichs said.

Frost and all-American Curt Pacha of Washington, Iowa, were something of exceptions in that they came from a distance to go to school. Friederichs, like Young at NIACC, did not have to go too far to find pools of wrestling talent to fish from. The programs at Humboldt, Eagle Grove, Clarion, Algona and Fort Dodge were all within fifty to sixty miles of campus and had individuals who could go to Division I as well as those who looked for a way to prepare for the top-line programs. Having a reputation of success at Iowa Central and such fertile recruiting turf nearby got things rolling at Iowa Central, Friederichs said.

"For that time, there were a lot of NCAA all-Americans coming out of those schools. That may not always get me a national championship team, but it ended up getting us one," Friederichs said. "The thing I was more concerned about with anything was whether they were going to leave the wrestling in Eagle Grove. I was commuting over there, and that's not good either, when you're not around during the day."

Friederichs said the wrestling was in Eagle Grove until the late 1970s, when a new training facility was built in Fort Dodge. There was a bit of a struggle because the folks in Eagle Grove didn't want to lose what they had, he said.

"I think the best thing I did, the most successful time I had, was getting third in the nationals when we were still at Eagle Grove. We had twenty-five wrestlers, and I don't think they had more than seventy-five or eighty kids in the whole school," Friederichs said. "That's why they really wanted me to keep going because it was improving their enrollment there. It was pretty hard to justify it when they had a nice, big new building over in Fort Dodge."

There had been some changes made, allowing students at Fort Dodge and Webster City to come to Eagle Grove to wrestle. That meant daily van rides to Eagle Grove from Fort Dodge. With the change to Fort Dodge came a new uniform and a new team moniker. Gone were the maroon-colored singlets of the Pirates and the blue-and-white uniforms of the Tritons. Friederichs was still there, getting guys ready to take on the nation.

"He enforced good, strong basics. Back then, you didn't have kids wrestling from kindergarten on, you didn't have youth programs, you probably didn't have much freestyle and Greco-Roman. Back then, pretty basic," Frost said. "I know strength was a big deal and, when you had something that worked that you were good at and strong enough to do it, it was solid. I don't recall learning anything above and beyond other than polishing and perfecting what you already knew."

Dave Morgan, a three-time state champion from Eagle Grove, was the first JUCO national champion in 1977. Another Eagle Grove wrestler, John Schaumburg, won nationals in 1980, and Kevin Russell of Clarion highlighted the team championship season of 1981 by winning an individual title. The 1979–80 and 1980–81 seasons were special, Frost said.

"We had a pretty good dang team those two years. It was more the guys getting on each other and getting going. Dennie didn't have to do it. He was there as support, a great guy and made decisions to help us out in the corner," Frost said. "It's kind of unique that Dennie coached teams as good as he did with his laid-back style. That was kind of hard to believe looking back on it right now. How did you make things happen in a good way? He just had that silent thing…expectations I guess. You just thought you were expected to do it, you did it. He didn't have to say much about it."

Most of the team that finished third in the 1980 tournament returned the following season. There may not have been considerable talk about what could happen in 1981, but the expectations were there. Frost sustained a high ankle sprain in his second tournament match as a sophomore and did not place.

"As many points and kids as we had coming back, we definitely had a great opportunity. It was back to what I said (earlier), we kind of helped each other and kept pushing. Dennie didn't have to say much because we just kind of knew what was on the line," Frost said. "You could just sense that all year long. We worked hard. We'd go to open tournaments, and we'd do very well against Division I wrestlers. It made sense if you look back on how many kids off that team wrestled at the Division I level. We knew everybody was going to have to do their job. I kind of feel like I fell short because I'd gotten fourth the year before as a freshman, and I was probably just about as in line as anybody on that team to be in the finals and even be a national champ that year until that injury."

Going into the 1981 tournament, Friederichs was a late arrival to the tournament site of Worthington, Minnesota. The funeral service for his father, Norman, was that day. As he drove north, Friederichs said he listened to the radio reports from the meet, and the outlook was not rosy. Iowa Central was ranked No. 1 nationally but qualified six of a possible ten wrestlers.

"We had the right six guys," Friederichs said. "I thought we had a chance of four champions. I thought that Al Frost would win it. He got injured in the nationals. I had Wayne Cole from Fort Dodge; he got in the finals, I thought he would win it. I wasn't sure about Russell. Russell was undefeated all year; everybody was telling me how great he was. He wasn't dominating all the time, but he was very consistent anyway. And I think Mark Ostrander, I thought he had a chance to win it. I guess you always think you've got a chance at winning if you have a decent team. I did actually do it. I felt like I accomplished something pretty important."

It was important enough that Iowa Central inducted the 1981 national champions into its athletics hall of fame.

"That, in a nutshell, sums it up. We wanted to be the ones more than anything else, make some history. That drives a guy—you're driven not only individually but you're driven as a team also," Frost said, recalling the cool time when the Tritons received the top trophy. "I do remember that moment. It was special. I didn't get my goals accomplished that year because I didn't place after being fourth the year before, but at the same time, it was a sense of accomplishment and a joyous opportunity that we had done it as a team. We did it. I'll never forget it. People ask me what my greatest memories in wrestling are, and I kind of reflect back on my Iowa Central years maybe more than anything else I had done. Making memories."

In order to have a team good enough to content for a national championship, a junior college coach has to recruit nearly nonstop. Friederichs said his wife, Jan, was key in that because she understood that reputation for quality had to be maintained. Aggressive scheduling helped the wrestlers be ready at tournament time, Friederichs said.

"You only have them for two years, so you've got to recruit a good bunch every year and for sure every two years," Friederichs said. "We always wrestled in the tough tournaments. We'd wrestle in the UNI tournament, Iowa State had a tournament back then, there was a big tournament in Omaha and you'd hit the Division I wrestlers so you got a pretty good idea of how you'd compete with them."

So, what kept Friederichs going through a lot of long weekends, the recruiting and being a husband and father? "I just loved wrestling so much," he said.

He was also in the hunt to bring another championship to Iowa Central. Friederichs said he thought a title was coming home in 1994, but Garden City Community College of Kansas took the gold and the Tritons were second.

"I thought we had the best chance of anybody to win it, and when they totaled the score up I had no idea that we would have lost because we had four guys in the finals," Friederichs said. "That's my only disappointment—that I couldn't get other national championships, but we were always pretty good."

There were a couple of instances where Friederichs submitted his resignation. One was when his son, Dennie, was wrestling at Fort Dodge High School and dad did not want to miss his son competing in the state tournament. The Iowa High School Athletic Association changed the date of its state tournament—it would not be at the same time as the JUCO tournament—and Friederichs took his job back.

A second resignation was tendered going into the 1988–89 season.

"I had a kid by the name of Paul Weltha. I heard talk of replacing me with somebody who had wrestled a little bit maybe in high school but wasn't a coach. I took it back, and they actually gave me a raise," Friederichs said. "The reason I mentioned Weltha, he was good, and I was sure he was going to be a national champion. He'd already been a runner-up so I thought I can't leave him with no coach."

Weltha, who was a state champion at Ames, was the national runner-up in 1988 and then won the national title in 1989. He went on to be an all-America football player at Western Illinois.

When Friederichs submitted his resignation and stayed resigned, he said the time was right to turn the program over to Ostrander.

"I think it was just getting so hard for me to go all day long on Saturdays and get home [at] one, two o'clock in the morning," Friederichs said. "It just kind of kept driving on me. I knew Mark wanted it pretty bad, so I figured it would be a good time to get out of it."

Before he left, Friederichs gave the program a cornerstone of success. Frost said he experienced a similar turning point with his program at Nashua-Plainfield. The Huskies won Class 1-A dual-meet state tournaments in 2004 and in 2012.

"I think we opened the door. It was kind of like what we had at Nashua-Plainfield for a while," Frost said. "Once we got that door opened in 2004, we finally won a state duals title, it kind of woke people up to realize it can be done. We continued that with a pretty dang good run of success."

Ostrander led the Tritons to the 2002 national championship, following two consecutive runner-up finishes. The 2002 title was decided in the final match. Cain Velasquez, a future world heavyweight champion in mixed martial arts, clinched the title with a 2–1 victory over Dean Taylor of Neosho Community College. Among Ostrander's recruits was a state champion from Estherville named Luke Moffitt. The 2000 national tournament saw Moffitt win a national championship. Four years later, Moffitt was named Iowa Central's coach. By 2006, Moffitt had the Tritons starting a run of what would become four consecutive team championships. Iowa Central added more team gold in 2015 and in 2017.

9
WAVERLY–SHELL ROCK'S RECORD

Big dreams early. Huge results later.

Eric Thompson remembered walking to Waverly–Shell Rock's junior high school with some friends, talking about what was to come. The walk was about one mile from the high school, after the kids had a morning workout with Tom Ballweg.

Tom Ballweg was a high school state champion at Sauk Prairie, Wisconsin, and he wrestled at University of Wisconsin. He had three sons—Matt, Mark and Jacob—who combined for seven state championships and a 501-21 record at Waverly–Shell Rock.

"I remember in seventh grade, we'd come in in the morning and Tom Ballweg would take us through a thirty-to-forty-minute drill before he had to go to work at Nestle," Thompson said. "Looking back, it's so cool that he was willing to dedicate that kind of time to help us get better at wrestling. Things like that made a difference. It was times like that when we'd go from the high school and we'd walk to the junior high that was a mile away. We'd talk about how good we were going to be in high school and how much better we were going to keep getting. Big dreams early."

The dream was that Waverly–Shell Rock would be home to a high school wrestling team for the ages in Iowa. In 2008—the start of a four-year run of traditional state championship team titles—the Go-Hawks scored an unprecedented 225 points in winning the Class 3-A championship.

Debating about the best moment of Iowa's traditional state wrestling tournament can have as many rounds as there has been years of

Growing Gold

Waverly–Shell Rock's team established the current state wrestling tournament record in 2008 by scoring 225 points in winning the Class 3-A championship. The team was inducted into the Hall of Fame of the National Wrestling Hall of Fame's Dan Gable Museum in Waterloo in 2019. *Courtesy of the Iowa High School Athletic Association.*

competition, but fans get to the point—or points—when arguing the best team. Waverly–Shell Rock's team gets the nod. In this age of analytics, numbers don't seem to lie.

"In high school, I believe we are (the best). Obviously, I'm biased, but you look at that team with what we accomplished and the guys that were a part of it," Cody Caldwell said. "Hey, 225 points has still yet to be touched. High school wrestling continues to develop and get better, but as it stands right now, that team was something special. It's a number that's going to be hard to touch."

Denver High School coach Chris Krueger added, "It's hard to argue with their talent. Top to bottom, that was an extremely talented team. They definitely did some really cool things with that group."

Southeast Polk coach Jason Christenson, whose team had a run of four straight titles denied by Fort Dodge in 2018, said one strategic difference between the 2008 mark and the present is the timing of the dual-meet state tournament. In 2012, the Iowa High School Athletic Association moved the date of the duals to the day before the traditional tournament when it moved the event to Des Moines from longtime host Cedar Rapids.

The Waverly–Shell Rock team set a state record by scoring 225 points in the 2008 Class 3-A state tournament. The record stands going into the 2019–20 season. In 2018, the team held a ten-year reunion at the Northeast Iowa Conference tournament in Waverly. Head coach Rick Caldwell (*third from left, back row*) welcomed home many of the wrestlers and the coaches from that team. *Photo by Dan McCool.*

"Going through a dual-meet tournament the day before now may make a difference in potential output of a group of guys. Obviously, they would have probably had to wrestle at least a couple of matches before the individual tournament started," Christenson said. "I see it, we've been in that situation. In 2012, we did not wrestle our state qualifiers, which was twelve of our guys or thirteen of our guys that year, in the duals. And then every year since we have. I can see by Saturday your kids have made weight four days in a row and been on an emotional roller coaster, so that may make a difference, that may be relative for us.

"That's not taking anything away from Coach Caldwell and the group of kids that he had. They came together and they wrestled lights-out at that tournament," Christenson added. "It would be like the '97 Hawkeyes. Is that relative today? It's something everybody's shooting for. It's a goal that we all have to try to beat it, so obviously it's relative but it still matters today. Some of those Dowling teams in that era, were they? I don't know what answers the best team. I think you start looking at the best team, and you've got to start looking at the state duals tournament."

What Waverly–Shell Rock did in the late 2000s, only two teams have exceeded. In 2008, Don Bosco of Gilbertville in Class 1-A was in the middle of a run of six consecutive traditional titles that started in 2005 and ended in 2010. Waterloo West was the first team with five consecutive championships between 1942 and 1946.

Growing Gold

The state duals, which debuted in 1987, was one week after the traditional tournament during Don Bosco's run, and the Dons reeled off six consecutive duals crowns. Former Don Bosco coach Tom Kettman said his predecessor, Dan Mashek, got the team thinking about being the best on the final night of competition.

"We've had our third- and fourth-place finishes, and most schools would think that's pretty good. We like to think that's an off year for us. Mashek preached that every year, I preached that, (Ray Fox) preached that: Our number one goal is to win the state title," Kettman said. "Then when we got a dual competition, our number one goal was to win two titles. We go into every season preaching that, and we really try to get the wrestlers to buy into it. We may not be here at the start of the season, but by the end of the year if they do what we suggest and work hard, we're going to be close."

Since 2008, only one team has cracked the 200-point mark at state. That was the Ballard of Huxley team scoring 220 in the 2009 meet. The Bombers set records for margin of victory (131.5 points) and most finalists (nine), and they have two of the top five team scores in tournament history.

A season of work hopefully culminates in a state championship for an Iowa high school wrestler. Doug Hatch of Dallas Center-Grimes jumped into the arms of head coach Andy Davidson after winning in the 1984 state tournament. Hatch's victory helped the Mustangs win the closest non-tie team race in tournament history—a margin of one-half point. *Photo by Thom Bartels.*

Waverly–Shell Rock added a sixth team championship to its collection in 2019 as Go-Hawk alum Eric Whitcome led the way as head coach. Southeast Polk was second, and Christenson found things to smile about after he, Whitcome and any other head coach in the state had numerous things to sweat and worry about every day during the season. One smile was Christenson's son, Gabe, winning his first state championship. Gabe was one month old when his father won his Southeast Polk coaching debut on November 29, 2001.

"It was worth it this year getting handed the silver trophy. That wasn't our goal, but having three champs, obviously having your own son win a title, just finishing the tournament that way on a positive note felt pretty good," Christenson said. "You're hurting for some of the guys who didn't get what they had set out for, but once again when you know that they gave their best effort and they did the things right makes it a lot easier to sleep at night and it makes you want to come back when you see kids achieve their goals, so then you get excited about the next go-round. This year at the individual, Waverly wrestled lights-out again, they were better than us, they had a great tournament, but it doesn't take away anything that our kids did. That's the relativity coming back around in a circle."

Southeast Polk beat Waverly–Shell Rock for the 2019 dual-meet state championship. The finishing touch for Southeast Polk was the announcement in June 2019 that Christenson was named National High School Coach of the Year by the National Wrestling Coaches Association.

Krueger led Denver-Tripoli to Class 2-A championships in 2010 and 2012. He came back home to Denver as coach for the 1999–2000 season—Krueger was a state qualifier for the Cyclones in 1990—and set out to fix what he said was a 0-15 record that had a carrot at the end of the proverbial string: strong future talent in a youth club. The Cyclones had a state qualifier in 1996, then went to Des Moines every other year in 2001, 2003 and a tide-turning 2005. Beginning with the three-man contingent of Cory Olson, Matt Chapman and Blake Hilmer in 2005, Krueger took qualifiers to state twelve of the next fourteen years. Krueger resigned his coaching duties prior to the 2019–20 season.

"It takes time. You've got to build that culture of families wanting to buy in, make it a fun experience where kids are getting better but families want to be a part of it," Krueger said. "When you travel somewhere and do something, nobody wants to feel left out, and they want to be a part of it. You can build that culture of that's the expectation, but it's not a grind, more of a fun experience for kids to be a part of and families want to be there."

GROWING GOLD

Wrestling can produce deep roots in a community with family involvement. Such is the case of the Sharp family of Ankeny, which was honored by Ankeny High School for a combined one hundred years of service to the school and its wrestling program. It all started with longtime head coach Bob Sharp. From left to right are Brian Sharp, Bob Sharp, Dave Sharp and Bob's grandson Ryan. *Photo by Dan McCool.*

The Denver fans cheered an individual state championship off and on between 1975 and 1995. Then they had a steady diet of winning between 2007 and 2016, with thirteen titles won by seven young men. Among that group was four-time champion Brandon Sorensen, three-time winner Dylan Peters and two-time champion Levi Wolfensperger.

"We wanted to show some success at the high school level, but we put a ton of time into just trying to build that culture through our youth program to get those families and kids excited," Krueger said. "We had some success at the high school level, more on the individual basis in those early years, but then as we got more and more kids involved and people wanting to be a part of it, that's kind of going back to that winning culture of putting the time in and doing all the right things. That's how we started building it up. As we got that group of families into the high school program, then we were able to toughen up our schedule and start going to some of the bigger tournaments. It's definitely a process."

Southeast Polk was trying to become only the sixth team to have at least four consecutive traditional championships in 2018. Emmetsburg is the lone program to win four in a row twice: once between 1976 and 1979 and then between 2000 and 2003 as Emmetsburg/Armstrong-Ringsted.

"It's harder than anybody realizes. There is so much more to it. The first time, even though I remember how spectacular that felt and to be like, 'Oh my goodness, that finally happened' after whatever it was for me, twenty-two years or something, then you realize just how good those teams that put four titles in a row together are," Christenson said. "A lot of things have to go right, and people can't forget everything that it took to get to that position. The more success you have, it's great that people have high expectations and they expect those things to happen, but they don't just happen. There is so much that goes into a championship season that most people aren't aware of, and then it just takes a little stumble or having a pebble in your shoe and stepping on it wrong and things can go haywire and off the rails. Those teams that can put it together and win like that, consistently and consecutively, that's all about the culture that you built but then also people remembering, 'We know what it was like when we weren't winning, and we don't want to go back there again.'"

Waverly–Shell Rock was happy to go back to the top in 2008. The Go-Hawks were three years removed from winning their first wrestling state championships, but the crowds had not dwindled. The 2005 squad won the traditional event and followed up by winning the dual-meet state tournament one week later. But if fans were impressed by that year and the 117-point accumulation, Cody Caldwell kept reminding people that the best was yet to come.

"We were already looking towards the future. I remember me and my buddies, Jake Ballweg, Jordan Rinken, Cody Krumwiede…we saw that, and we were like, 'Just wait, just wait,'" said Caldwell, whose dad, Rick, was the head coach of the Go-Hawks. "That made us even more eager to get there so that we have an opportunity to perform and show what we were capable of. We knew it was going to be something special; it was just a matter of time."

The youth program in Waverly is known as Waverly Area Wrestling Club. Early in the twenty-first century, some special dads, including Jerome Rinken, Ron Krumwiede and Bill Thompson, were helping Ballweg coach kids and also pitching in to drive to wherever the good youth tournaments were. They were more than just there until their sons graduated, Cody recalled.

"It started early, I'd say fifth or sixth grade, when all of the dads started traveling around the country to take us to different events. It wasn't like they were just at practice for their son or whatever. It was to develop the whole team, and they had a vested interest in us," Cody said. "That was noticeable, that was realized at a young age. Maybe at that time I didn't realize it, but looking back this was all planned for us to work extremely hard, stay together, travel the country, wrestle in as many competitions as we could and to get the very most out of us so then once we hit ninth grade, we were bound and ready to have the best team that the state of Iowa's ever seen."

A band of kids who could have been all over the town and parts of Bremer County playing baseball, swimming, fishing and boating were in the practice room doing takedowns and keeping each other in check.

"It was kids at a young age helping each other hold each other accountable," Eric Thompson said. "If you missed a lift or a drill or something, it wasn't that you were afraid you were going to get yelled at by Coach Caldwell, it was that you were going to get made fun of by the other guys on the team or they were going to tell you, 'Why weren't you there?' and you had to come up with an excuse or you just had to take it on the chin."

What was worse? Coach Caldwell ripping into you or your buddies doing the ripping?

"That's a tight race right there. It was a no-win situation for either of them," Eric said. "You'll get over Coach Caldwell getting mad at you, but sometimes when it's the team, it's like, 'Oh man, this sucks.'"

Waverly and parts of Northeast Iowa were getting more and more fired up about the sport of wrestling because Wartburg was frequently winning the NCAA Division III championship and rarely lost a dual meet. Rick Caldwell came to Waverly from Ames High School for the 1998–99 season to be an assistant under Jim Miller at Wartburg. The Knights won their second national title. Caldwell then was hired at Waverly–Shell Rock for the 1999–2000 season, and in 2005 he directed the Go-Hawks to the top of the big school mountain.

"There was some excitement already in the town of Waverly with Wartburg and the dynasty that they were building. When my dad first got there, Waverly was not even in the picture of being a state trophy contender, but I know from the start that's what he wanted to do," Cody said. "It took a little time, and in the end he got it done. Two extremely successful programs that have a very rich history now, that's very cool."

When Rick took the job at Wartburg, Cody was in first grade. "I remember I had some friends that lived on my corner. I was pretty upset having to leave some of them," Cody admitted, "but I'm still very close to my family and I did what I was told, so it was time to go. It couldn't have been a better situation for me."

Part of the deal was being exposed to a motivator such as Miller, best known as Milboy.

"With my dad spending a year there, he really looked to Milboy as a mentor," Cody said. "Even I still look to Milboy. I'm coaching at South Dakota State, and I'll give Milboy a call to pick his brain on some things."

A coach's son who would develop big dreams of his own could not have asked for a better new place to call home. Thompson said the dads knew there was more than just wins and losses to the youth club.

"It's a lot of dads who were very passionate about wrestling, saw the value in it for their sons, not just winning and losing but teaching their kid hard work and resiliency in life," Thompson said. "I think they did have a little more forward-thinking view. For me, my dad didn't really care about winning and losing all that much. It was more about the way I competed and the effort I gave. If I put my head down and someone ran behind me, that was the most mad he ever got. If I got beat by ten points but I fought the whole time, then he didn't get mad. I think that was all the dads at Waverly. I think every dad or every coach, you lose track sometimes of what the message is. There was always somebody there that kind of reaffirmed the message of keep getting better."

Thompson and the 2008 seniors were freshmen when the 2005 titles came home with the Go-Hawks. Whatever they learned about leadership then, they implemented in the 2007–8 season when Cody was a freshman.

"Our guys that were seniors on that team—Mark Ballweg, Eric Thompson, Anthony Campbell and Matt Kittleson—those guys didn't let us young guys forget it that we had something to prove," Cody said. "When we stepped on the mat, we were representing more than just ourselves. We were representing Waverly-Shell Rock wrestling and this community. That's something I really believe is special. It was something that was developed over a long time, and to get in that position and be able to represent this community that had done so much for us, it was really a privilege. So, we knew that every time we stepped on the mat that what was behind us was stronger than what was in front of us. Fortunately, we were able to put together a hell of a season and finish as the best team that Iowa's ever seen."

What was ahead of them was at times a daunting challenge—for example, the trip to Rochester, Minnesota, for a tournament known as "The Clash." That tournament draws tough teams from all over the country. Teams with undefeated records go there to take a hit or two. Waverly-Shell Rock, which was ranked No. 5 by *Amateur Wrestling News* at the time, beat two of three top-10 teams on the final day of the event and won the team title on criteria—sportsmanship.

The Go-Hawks beat No. 9 Glenbard North and No. 7 Montini Catholic, both of Illinois, and lost to No. 4 Apple Valley of Minnesota. Waverly–Shell Rock, Montini and Apple Valley were all 2-1 in that round-robin session, but the Go-Hawks were the only one of the three not to lose a team point for unsportsmanlike conduct, so that was the No. 1 criteria.

Waverly–Shell Rock prepared for such tough meets by facing 2007 Class 3-A state champion Iowa City West at the Five Seasons Duals in Cedar Rapids—a 39–33 victory that ended West's thirty-five-meet winning streak—and Class 1-A powerhouse Don Bosco of Gilbertville, which was in the midst of winning five consecutive championships. A 36–15 win halted Don Bosco's winning streak at ninety-two, the state's second-longest run of success. "The Clash" opened the January schedule and was perhaps a postdated Christmas present.

"It was a pretty special tournament. For us to win a national event like that was something that hadn't happened often," Cody said of "The Clash" success. "I don't know if any other team in Iowa had done that. It definitely put people on notice. At that point we were thinking, 'We have a chance to win a national title as a team.' That's pretty crazy to even consider. For us to go and win that tournament against the elite was pretty special."

Waverly–Shell Rock and Apple Valley met a second time that season in Waverly as a prelude to the Wartburg-Augsburg college dual. Apple Valley won, the only team to beat Waverly–Shell Rock (25–2) that season.

In Iowa, Class 3-A teams hope to have their skills honed to a sharp edge by district tournament time. That's the qualifier for the state tournament, and it was getting time to see what the Go-Hawk machine was going to do. By then, Waverly–Shell Rock was No. 4 nationally. Led by eleven district champions, the Go-Hawks moved thirteen (one short of a full lineup) to state. No competition at the district? Well, future two-time NCAA champion Matt McDonough was there for Linn-Mar of Marion, and future NCAA champion Kyven Gadson of Waterloo East finished second to Michael Kelly of Cedar Falls, a future starter for Iowa. Waverly–Shell Rock totaled a stunning 313.5 points, well ahead of the 155 points by runner-up Waterloo East. Eric Thompson, the No. 1 big man in the country, was one week away from winning his second state championship at heavyweight. He would go on to win three NAIA national championships at Grand View University in Des Moines.

Cody had big goals in mind as a freshman, even before he earned his first trip to state as a 112-pounder. He would finish fourth.

"I'm pretty satisfied, happy, with the experience I had on that team. It was the only year I didn't win a state title, but it was *the* most rewarding and fun experience that I had in high school," Cody said. "The whole season, my individual goal was to be a state champ. Going into high school, I wanted to be a four-time state champ. I'd seen guys do it before me. I believe that I was capable, and I came up short, but it definitely was the greatest experience that I had in high school just because of the leadership that we had. I'm surrounded by guys I really looked up to, and I was able to be a part of their team. To go out and put on that singlet and represent week in, week out, it was extremely fun. I look back on that season and I have a ton of great memories from that 2007–8 year. I was surrounded by some incredible individuals. Not saying that our teams after that weren't, we won the traditional state title every year that I was in high school, but that team was something special. The leadership, the camaraderie, the way we were able to come together and put together a great performance was something that was very rewarding."

When they got to Wells Fargo Arena in Des Moines for the state meet, the Go-Hawks wrestled as if they got their energy from a buffet of bonus points.

"It escalated very quickly as far as points go. All of a sudden we're sitting in the back, one guy comes back and he's like, 'I got a major' and another guy came back, 'I teched a kid,'" Thompson said. "It was like one guy after another after another and you're like, 'When was the last time we lost?'"

Cockiness? That might have been shared for the most private of team moments. Nothing was shared.

"I think when we were with each other, we would kind of get the cockiness out of our systems then. When it came time to compete, it was just go compete, not much to be said about it," Thompson said. "I think that's a testament to how we were raised and the place we grew up in. It's not always about how much you can talk, but sometimes it's more about how long can you work, how much can you do."

Cody and his freshmen teammates helped send the 2008 seniors out in golden style, then had their own run of success by hoisting the championship trophy every year they were in school—adding 2009, 2010 and 2011. It seems difficult to pick one title as better than the others, but Cody said the 2008 gold was a prized vintage.

"It is hard, but that (2008) team was special. It's hard to even describe how special in the fact we had all grown up together in the Waverly Area Wrestling Club, we had grown up going to tournaments, we had practiced, worked, dedicated our time and effort for years and years," Cody said.

"Ever since 2005, we were looking towards that 2007–8 team. We knew we were going to have that team where that great group of seniors was going to be there and my class as freshmen was going to be there as well. One year on the same team, we knew it was going to be special and that's exactly what it was.

"I think that was kind of the whole plan my dad and staff had in place. They wanted to get us younger guys around the program, so we knew what it took to be successful at an early age. We trained with those high school guys as much as possible. Don't get me wrong, we got our butts kicked sometimes, but it was preparing us for that year. Looking back, I may not have realized it then, but my dad, maybe he is kind of smart. He had a plan, having us all around the program and around those guys because that year when we stepped into the lineup we were ready. Some guys may go the other way, but we were ready, we were focused and excited about what was to come with WSR wrestling."

Krueger said the desire to do big things on a regular basis can be a touch frustrating, such as for Denver at the 2019 state tournament.

"We had a school-record ten state qualifiers, a school-record eight state placers but we got second, and it felt like a miserable season," Krueger said. "We got our program to where the gold standard is the gold. That part's good, but at the same time you've got to take a step back sometimes and realize what good things you are doing and look at what some of the kids were able to accomplish on an individual level. This sport's weddings and funerals, you've just got to build on those weddings a little bit more I guess."

In 2008, when they finally stopped winning matches that weekend, the Go-Hawks were able to celebrate. Father and son Caldwell got to have a moment.

"Not a lot of words were spoken. It was more of a realization that something special had just occurred," Cody said. "It took a little while to kind of really understand what that team had just accomplished. He gave me a hug, he said he was proud of me and he said, 'That was a pretty special team that Waverly-Shell Rock just put on the mat, I'm grateful you were able to be a part of it.'"

The Go-Hawks held a ten-year reunion of the 2008 champions on the same day they played host to the Northeast Iowa Conference tournament. There were legends in the crowd, such as three-time state champion and NCAA all-American Mark Sindlinger of Charles City and state and NCAA champion Tom Peckham of Cresco, but the longest salute was given to the record breakers. Cody had to miss the event because he was helping head coach Chris Bono coach the South Dakota State University wrestling team on a road trip to Oklahoma. Thompson made it back from Pennsylvania and gave a speech. He spoke of how important that mark was, how it was a big deal and how it's still a big deal.

"People dedicated their lives to have something like that, to get the end product that we had gotten," Thompson said. "It was pretty incredible."

Krueger said topping Waverly–Shell Rock's record will be difficult with a team that has stayed together for a long time, as the Go-Hawks did. The growth in open enrollment and in families willing to move to a different school district has cut into those hopes.

"Like anything else in life, people always think it's greener somewhere else," Krueger said. "It definitely has changed the game, changed the sport. Kids getting to meet other kids at clubs has really changed the sport. They want to wrestle with like-minded kids. The super clubs are now trying to become the super teams at the high school level."

There have been some dominant teams throughout the history of Iowa's state tournament. The stories go back to 1921, when Iowa State College put on an invitational event that occurred one floor apart from a swimming meet. Cedar Rapids High School (now known as Cedar Rapids Washington)

The Northeast Iowa Conference tournament is billed as Iowa's oldest high school conference meet. The 2018 meet brought together some legendary individuals who wrestled, coached or officiated in the event. From left to right are Tom Peckham of Cresco, Arlo Flege of Waverly, Jim Miller of Charles City and Bill Roths of New Hampton. *Photo by Dan McCool.*

took home the team honors. One of the coaches on that team was Martin "Farmer" Burns, a nineteenth-century heavyweight champion wrestler in the "catch-as-catch-can" style who trained eventual world champion Frank Gotch of Humboldt along with heavyweight champion Earl Caddock of Walnut and middleweight champion Ralph Parcaut of Sutherland.

In 1924, Marshalltown had arguably the best tournament showing by an Iowa high school wrestling team. The meet was at Iowa City, as University of Iowa staged a tournament much as its Ames counterpart did. There were nine weight classes, eight of them contested, and Marshalltown finished with eight champions and one runner-up effort. Marshalltown heavyweight Eugene Fitz was the sole entrant in his division. The historic part of the tournament was that future Olympic gold medalist Allie Morrison won the 125-pound championship and was considered by the school as its wrestling coach, the first time a wrestler won an individual laurel as well as a team title.

The Iowa High School Athletic Association began sanctioning the wrestling tournament in 1926, and Marshalltown was its first champion. Morrison was the coach and future National Collegiate Basketball Hall of Fame coach Adolph Rupp was the faculty advisor. Morrison could not compete because he was twenty years old, making him ineligible as an athlete.

Fort Dodge became the first traditional power of the IHSAA-era tournament, winning seven championships and sharing an eighth with Eldora Training School between 1927 and 1937. The coach was Fred Cooper, who led sixteen men to a total of nineteen state titles during that run. The Gargano brothers Joe, Frank and Tony were state champions, and their brother William finished second. Frank (1929) and Tony Gargano (1930) each won a national championship at a tournament in Evanston, Illinois, and Frank was joined by teammate Lyle Sells. Another national champion was Dale Brand, who in 1937 became the first NCAA champion for Cornell College in Mount Vernon, Iowa. All told, twenty-five Fort Dodge wrestlers totaled twenty-eight championships between 1926 and 1942.

Andrew Pontius, who joined Joe Gargano as the Dodgers' champion in 1927, became a good example of how tough the kids were who called themselves "Coop's Boys." A car taking some of the Fort Dodge wrestlers to the state meet in Ames broke down. Some were picked up by another vehicle, but others walked an estimated six to seven miles to get to Boone, where they would take a train to Ames to be there in time for weigh-ins. Pontius got a case of frostbite bad enough to cause an ear to swell up and split, but he won the 158-pound championship.

Waterloo began to serve as the epicenter of Iowa's high school wrestling hotbeds in the 1940s and stayed there through the 1960s. The city's West High won five consecutive team championships between 1942 and 1946, thanks to the coaching work of Finn Eriksen and Roy Jarrard. Eriksen led the Wahawks to their championships in 1942 and 1943, and Jarrard followed him with titles in 1944, 1945 and 1946. They are two of the state's four coaches who have led two different schools to state championships: Eriksen at New Hampton (tying with New Hampton in 1933) and Jarrard at Cherokee (1939). The other two are Ron Peterson of Clarksville (1991) and Cedar Rapids Prairie (1995) and Brad Smith of Lisbon (1980, 1982–83, 1986, 1988–90, 2017 and 2018) and Iowa City High (1992, 1999 and 2002).

West and crosstown East combined for seven team championships during the 1950s and another eight during the 1960s. The '50s saw Bob Siddens begin his eleven-championship coaching run at West in 1951 and Dave Natvig get his first of seven titles at East in 1953. At the time, Waterloo was known for its strong labor force at places such as John Deere tractors or Rath Packing.

"It was just a tough, blue-collar city. The work ethic that the people had was a large factor," said Jim Duschen, a wrestler at East who went on to earn all-America honors at Iowa State before embarking on a Hall of Fame coaching career in Nevada. "Great coaches. Wrestlers were highly respected during that era, so a lot of youngsters coming up, they wanted to wrestle because they knew wrestlers were respected. There was a lot of interest, and they were just tough, hard-nosed kids."

Iowa's best-known wrestling product, Dan Gable, won three state championships and never lost in sixty-four high school bouts for West. He won two NCAA championships, lost his only college or high school bout in the 1970 NCAA finals, won a world championship in freestyle in 1971 and then put forth what many say is the best Olympic effort by an American wrestler: he won gold in 1972 without giving up a point.

Waterloo's three high schools—Columbus is a parochial school—have graduated ten individuals who won NCAA Division I championships. The number goes to eleven if Joe Gibbons of Iowa State is included. Gibbons, a four-time state champion, won his first two prep titles at Columbus before moving to Ames, where he won the last two. Gable (1969) and Chuck Yagla of Columbus (1976) were voted Outstanding Wrestler of the NCAA meet.

The state of Iowa has had twelve of its high school graduates win the Outstanding Wrestler honor thirteen times (Bill Koll of Fort Dodge and Iowa State Teachers College was the first wrestler to win it consecutively in

State champion wrestlers in Iowa grow up to have children who win state championships. Gary Steffensmeier of Fort Madison (*left*) was a two-time champion. His son, Harlan, won a state title for Fort Madison in 2018 and is now wrestling at the Air Force Academy. *Photo by Dan McCool.*

1947 and 1948) in the Division I tournament, beginning with Dale Hanson of Cresco in 1939 while wrestling at University of Minnesota. In addition, 2006 "OW" (Outstanding Wrestler) winner Ben Askren of Missouri was born in Cedar Rapids.

Waterloo East had perhaps its brightest moment in tournament time in 1964, when the Trojans qualified five wrestlers and won five championships. That success, plus a victory by Kent Osboe of Fort Dodge over Bud Knox of West in the heavyweight finale gave East the championship by one point over West.

Northeast Iowa hosted the state tournament twenty-two times between 1933 and 1969. It moved to Des Moines in 1970 and, except for one year in Ames in 1971, has been in the Capital City since. Cedar Falls hosted thirteen times, including 1962. That was when Bob Steenlage of Britt became the first Iowan to annex four state championships.

Other Northeast Iowa schools that were major players at state were New Hampton, which tied Cresco for the 1933 crown and then added titles in 1957, 1959, 1963, 1990 and 1993; Cresco, with seven; Cedar Falls, with

A History of Wrestling in Iowa

The ultimate goal of a high school wrestler in Iowa is to win four state championships. Bob Steenlage of Britt became the first four-timer in 1962. Going into the 2019–20 season, there are twenty-seven four-time champions. *Courtesy of Bob Steenlage.*

five; and Don Bosco, with eleven. New Hampton has had five different coaches—Eriksen, Gene Luttrell, John Philo, Frank Powell and Arlin Severson—lead the championship charge. Cresco had two titles under the direction of Dave Bartelma, who would later become wrestling coach at University of Minnesota and be recognized as the father of high school wrestling in Minnesota. Also, Cresco had a third-place wrestler in 1932 named Norman Borlaug, who received the 1970 Nobel Peace Prize for his work in making strains of wheat that withstood harsh conditions and prevented the starvation of more than one billion people. Borlaug is one of only seven people in the world to have received the Nobel Peace Prize, the Presidential Medal of Freedom and the Congressional Gold Medal.

Cedar Falls had championship coaches in Keith Young and Gene Doyle, two men who never competed in the state tournament but knew how to pull big things out of their athletes. Young was a three-time NCAA champion at Iowa State Teachers College.

Don Bosco of Gilbertville is a small parochial school that has had three official coaches and nearly nine hundred dual-meet victories to go with eleven state championships since the 1970–71 campaign. The program's first coach

Veterans Memorial Auditorium in Des Moines was the place to be for wrestling fans for nearly thirty-five years. The building, known by its moniker "The Barn," played host to the state tournament in 1970 and then annually between 1972 and 2005. *Courtesy of the Iowa High School Athletic Association.*

was a University of Northern Iowa student named John Maehl, who said he was paid six dollars a day in the beginning. Because Maehl did not have full coaching authorization, the Dons did not have a true varsity program until Dan Mashek was hired for the 1970–71 season. Mashek wrestled for Bob Siddens at Waterloo West and for Chuck Patten at Northern Iowa. He was also elected mayor of Gilbertville and served as head coach for thirty seasons. Mashek, once Iowa's leader in coaching wins, was 421-69-5 with four traditional and one dual-meet championship at Don Bosco. That set the table for coaches Tom Kettman and Tom Hogan, who followed Mashek as the Dons' coach, as well as Ray Fox, the program's first state champion who still helps with the team.

"We've had our third- and fourth-place finishes, and most schools would think that's pretty good. We like to think that's an off year for us," said Kettman, who led Don Bosco to seven dual-meet titles and five consecutive traditional top trophies after Mashek went to North Scott of Eldridge. "Mashek preached that every year, I preached that, Crazy Ray preached that: Our number one goal is to win the state title. Then when we got a dual competition, our number one goal is to win two titles. We go into every

In 1979, Don Bosco of Gilbertville became the most recent team to qualify its entire lineup for the state wrestling tournament. At that time, there were twelve weight classes. The Dons were coached by Dan Mashek (*back row, far right*), who was the first Iowa high school coach to record four hundred dual meet wins. *Courtesy of the Iowa High School Athletic Association.*

season preaching that, and we really try to get the wrestlers to buy into it. We may not be here at the start of the season, but by the end of the year if they do what we suggest and work hard, we're going to be close."

Hogan led the team to its most recent championships in the 2019 dual-meet and traditional tournaments.

Don Bosco holds a bit of history in that Mack Reiter and Bart Reiter became the first brothers to win four state championships. Mack won his four between 2000 and 2003, and Bart followed with a quartet between 2006 and 2009.

Don Bosco's rival is Lisbon, which is located east of Cedar Rapids. The Lions put their sixteenth traditional championship trophy in the school display case in 2018, and their dual meets against Don Bosco draw standing-room-only crowds that rival what the rivalries of old commanded.

Al Baxter lit the fire with five championships between 1973 and 1978 prior to becoming wrestling coach at NCAA Division III Buena Vista College in Storm Lake. His replacement was Brad Smith, a two-time state champion in Illinois who was an NCAA champion at Iowa. Smith won nine titles in two stints at Lisbon between 1980 and 2018. Between those stops, he led Iowa City High to championships in 1992, 1999 and 2002.

Smith's twelve championships put him one ahead of Siddens for the state's most coaching titles in the sport. One more traditional championship for the Lions and they tie Waterloo West's mark of seventeen gold trophies. Smith has coached some or all of the careers of

The cover of the first issue of *The Predicament*, a publication devoted to Iowa's wrestling scene. The publication was sold at the 1970 state tournament to see if there was interest in such an enterprise. Enough money was made to pay for the next edition, and it's the oldest of any state's wrestling publication in the United States. *Courtesy of John Doak.*

Scott Morningstar, Shane Light and Carter Happel at Lisbon and Jeff McGinness at Iowa City High. He may have a fifth one in Cael Happel, Carter's brother, who is after a fourth title in the 2019–20 season. Smith became the second coach to have two four-timers from start to finish with Light and Carter Happel.

Davenport does not boast of a mat full of championship trophies (it won in 1954 and 1956 before additional schools opened and Davenport High became Davenport Central), but it has some sterling representatives on the mat. In 1954, Simon Roberts became Iowa's first African American state champion. Future fifteen-term member of the United States House of Representatives Jim Leach won a gold medal in 1960.

In 1957, Roberts also became the first black wrestler to win an NCAA Division I championship, while wrestling at University of Iowa.

Davenport Central graduate Roger Craig was a state qualifier in 1977 and 1978 who earned three Super Bowl championships with the San Francisco 49ers. Craig was named NFL "Offensive Player of the Year" in 1988.

The first coach to coach the career of two four-time winners was Brian Reimers of Ogden, who worked with Jason Keenan and Jesse Sundell. Both wrestlers lost only once in their careers. Sundell, who nearly had his career cut short by a horrific rodeo accident, was beaten by Mario Galanakis of Nodaway Valley of Greenfield. Keenan's loss was by injury default when an opponent's injury was caused by Keenan's illegal hold.

Emmetsburg did not make headlines until the late '70s, but those were big. The E'Hawks had a run of four consecutive championships between 1976 and 1979 under the direction of Bob Roethler, who survived a brain aneurysm at the start of the 1978–79 season to be able to see the team hoist the fourth trophy. That run coincided with the state's second four-time state champion: Emmetsburg's Jeff Kerber, who was 126-0 and scored his 100th career pin in his fourth title match.

Clint Young, a member of the traditionally strong Algona program and a nephew of three-time NCAA champion Keith Young, led Emmetsburg to championships in 1982 and 1985. Bob Kenny added a half-dozen titles between 2000 and 2006 as the E'Hawks shared their program with nearby Armstrong-Ringsted and once again built a Class 2-A powerhouse.

In recent years, Southeast Polk has emerged as a force in the big-school class. The Rams won their first traditional trophy in 2013, then added more in 2015, 2016 and 2017. In 2018, Fort Dodge halted the Rams' run of success and Waverly–Shell stymied them the following year. Jason Christenson has helmed all the Southeast Polk championships, putting his

Winning four state titles is difficult. Winning every high school match is harder. Jeff Kerber of Emmetsburg, shown with some of his treasures, became Iowa's second four-time state champion in 1979. He was 126-0 and scored his 100th career pin in his final match. *Photo by Dan McCool.*

family in rare company. His father, Denny Christenson, led Belle Plaine to a championship in 1976. They are the second father-son coaching combo to win gold, joining Marv and Mark Reiland.

Marv coached Eagle Grove to state championships in 1974, 1986 and 1987. Mark directed Iowa City West to the top in 2006 and 2007.

Bob Darrah won four state championships at West Des Moines Dowling, but he engineered the start of a formidable record that still stands as the 2019–20 season dawns. The Maroons won 136 dual meets in a row between January 25, 1986, and January 4, 1992. Darrah, whose teams at Morning Sun, Urbandale and Dowling lost a total of seventeen meets, retired as a high school coach after the 1988–89 season. He was succeeded by longtime assistant Ron Gray, who won a pair of traditional titles.

Darrah was head coach of Iowa's freestyle delegation to the Junior Nationals tournament from 1971 to 1989, and the state had at least one national champion every year until 1988. Under Darrah's leadership, the Iowa team won the mythical national team championship nine times (1974, 1978–84 and in 1987). Iowa also won a national team title in 2008.

Iowa also won two mythical (1984 and 2002) and one official national team championship (2006) in Greco-Roman. Iowa is No. 1 in Junior Nationals freestyle championships with sixty-five and is tied with Illinois for the most top-five team finishes with thirty-four. Iowa also won an unofficial Cadet Nationals team title in 1987 and an official Cadet Greco-Roman championship in 2006.

Iowa had four Cadet Greco-Roman champions in 2006, which shares a record with five other states. Its seven Greco-Roman champions overall in 2006 shares a record with Illinois. Individually, David Kjeldgaard of Council Bluffs Lewis Central has a share of three records: most overall championships (eight), total medals (eleven) and most Greco-Roman medals (six). Mark Schwab of Osage shares a record for most finals appearances in Junior Nationals freestyle with four.

The Junior Nationals began in Iowa City in 1972 and was in Cedar Falls before moving to Warrensburg, Missouri, and St. Paul. It moved to Fargo

No wrestling official in Iowa worked as many state tournaments as Jim Christensen of Fontanelle. Christensen retired after the 2019 tournament, which was his thirty-fifth on the whistle. *Photo by Dan McCool.*

in 1993, and the Cadet Nationals joined it there in 1996. The girls' Junior Nationals started in Fargo in 2002, and the girls' Cadet Nationals started in 2011. Iowa ranks sixth in overall all-Americans with 903 and in overall national champions with 144, according to Jason Bryant's *USA Wrestling Junior and Cadet Nationals All-American Almanac*.

10
GIRLS' WRESTLING

No one is sure when the first female wrestled in a high school varsity match in Iowa, but the sport continues to grow, as some notable efforts have already been logged.

Grand View University in Des Moines is starting a women's wrestling program in the 2019–20 season. Iowa Wesleyan of Mount Pleasant, Indian Hills Community College of Ottumwa/Centerville and William Penn University of Oskaloosa will start a women's and men's program in the 2020–21 season. That will give Iowa five colleges offering such an activity. Waldorf College (now Waldorf University) in Forest City began its program in the 2010–11 season. There were 149 girls out for wrestling in Iowa's high schools in December 2018. That number jumped to 189 after it was announced that Waverly would play host to a girls-only tournament in January 2019. The tournament was sponsored by the Iowa Wrestling Coaches and Officials Association but not sanctioned by the Iowa Girls High School Athletic Union or the Iowa High School Athletic Association, so not an official state tournament.

Sanctioning by the IGHSAU will take some time for any new sport, according to Executive Director Jean Berger. The next sport could be wrestling or archery, lacrosse, rugby, shooting sports or competitive cheer, she said. The girls' union, like the IHSAA, requires 15 percent of the member schools—roughly fifty—to offer the sport and request sanctioning.

In the summer of 2019, eighteen states sanctioned girls' wrestling. Missouri was the lone state bordering Iowa among that group, according to information from the National Wrestling Coaches Association.

Ali Gerbracht of AGWSR of Ackley, shown going for a takedown in action during the 2018–19 season, won the first championship of the first all-girls wrestling tournament staged during the regular season in Iowa. *Photo by Dan McCool.*

"If enough of our member schools want to add the sport and offer it to girls, they would petition our board for an approval process that we go through," Berger said. "I would guess anywhere between two and three years, and that's just based on gathering information, getting venues, setting up rules, giving schools time to hire coaches and get schedules, get their interest built up. You don't say, 'Here's a tournament' the next week and do it well. How are we going to qualify? How many weight classes? Whether we're going to use (freestyle) or (folkstyle), what do we do about officials, even what season should it be in?"

The most recent individual wrestling accomplishment was turned in by Ali Gerbracht, a junior at AGWSR High School of Ackley. Historical and perhaps an answer to a trivia question, but it could be said she's just following the suggestion of her head coach.

On January 18, 2019, Gerbracht, a 106-pounder for the school that combines Ackley, Geneva, Wellsburg and Steamboat Rock, became the first individual champion of a girls' wrestling tournament staged in Iowa during the regular season. She was later announced as the first recipient of the "Ms. Wrestler" award, which carries the name of Olympic gold medalist Dan

Ali Gerbracht of AGWSR of Ackley goes over some last-minute technique with her head coach and father, Chad, during the 2018–19 season. She is on track to become the second female in Iowa high school wrestling to win one hundred career matches during the 2019–20 season. *Photo by Dan McCool.*

Gable, who has become a strong booster of women's wrestling. The head coach at AGWSR is her father, Chad Gerbracht.

There were some pioneering girls in Iowa going back to the early 1990s prior to Gerbracht's effort. They were people such as Atina Bibbs of Davenport Central and Stacy Light of Lisbon, Heather Morley of Urbandale, Cindy Johnson of West Burlington–Notre Dame, Tiffany Sluik of Mason City and Ashley Pender of Colfax-Mingo, who left their mark without an in-season girls' tournament. Bibbs beat Light in what is believed to be Iowa's first high school match between two girls on February 2, 1993. Morley was the first to win a match in either the traditional state tournament or the dual-meet state tournament in the 2005 dual-meet event. In 2011, Cassy Herkelman of Cedar Falls was the first girl to qualify for the state wrestling tournament, and Megan Black of Ottumwa became the second qualifier minutes later at another district. Black transferred to Eddyville-Blakesburg-Fremont and became the first girl to earn a medal, placing eighth in the 2012 Class 1-A event. Rachel Watters of Ballard of Huxley never made it to state but qualified for the 2016 Olympic trials, won three national championships (two in juniors, one at the cadet level) at Fargo and wrestled on two of her three Junior World teams while in high school.

Black and Watters won sectional championships—the first step for Class 1-A and Class 2-A wrestlers trying to qualify for state. Class 3-A schools do not have a sectional. Pender (in 2003) and Johnson (in 2004) competed in district tournaments after finishing top-two in their sectionals, and Sluik was a varsity regular prior to earning all-America honors at Jamestown College in North Dakota. In 2018, Felicity Taylor of South Winneshiek High School in Calmar became the state's first female to win 100 matches, won "Outstanding Wrestler" honors at the Girls' Junior Nationals in Fargo and was ranked No. 1 nationally during her first season of college at McKendree University in Lebanon, Illinois, during the 2018–19 season. Alanah Vetterick of Norwalk earned all-America honors for Midland University of Nebraska in the first NAIA women's wrestling tournament in 2019.

"I like being a part of history. It's really cool," Ali said. "The amount of support from this sport is just amazing."

Chad Gerbracht added, "We tell our kids on Day One when they come in as freshmen, 'Go make a name for yourself, a name that people are going to remember.' Well, she did that this (season), so that's outstanding."

In Waverly on that snowy Saturday in January, Ali beat Ella Schmit of Bettendorf 4–1 for the championship. That tournament had eighty-seven participants, a number reduced by inclement weather that weekend. Berger

Felicity Taylor (*top*) of South Winneshiek High School in Calmar became the first female in Iowa high school wrestling to win one hundred matches. She was a three-time Upper Iowa Conference champion and earned all-America honors in her first season of college wrestling in 2019. *Photo by Dan McCool.*

was in attendance. Iowa is the only state that has a separate governing office for girls' sports. Also in attendance was Watters, who has twice earned all-America honors wrestling at Oklahoma City University.

"I think it's awesome. I didn't think it was going to come this soon," Watters said. "When I was wrestling, I knew of Megan Black and Cassy Herkelman, and that's it. I would go to tournaments all year long and I wouldn't see anybody, and I'd maybe see Megan at state. I think it's so, so, so cool and so crazy that it's going this fast, but awesome at the same time. I was talking to my dad about it, and I was like, 'You know what? When I have kids and I have grandkids, there's probably going to be a point where girls that wrestle are going to be like, 'Oh wait, you wrestled when it wasn't even a D-1 sport?' I can't wait for that day. People are going to think it's crazy when I'm older, that I wrestled on an all-boys team at Ballard in Central Iowa."

Berger was struck by the athleticism of the competitors at Waverly and had other parts of the day to review. "My observations were there were some coaches who were in there coaching (hard) and they were all-in, and then there were others who maybe weren't as into it. Maybe that's just their coaching personality," Berger said. "It was hard for me to know who was there to watch just the girls because they had a boys' wrestling tournament. I thought they did a good job of showcasing them on the middle mat—I think Charlotte [Bailey] had something to do with that—and awarding them so they made it special for them. I was also struck by the amount of varying opinions you got on certain things based on who you talked to.

"There was a parent of a young girl, he was a former youth wrestling coach, and he told me flat-out we've got to do folkstyle rules," Berger said. "When I ask officials, (they say) the only way to go is freestyle. Why? Because our officials know those rules. What's best for the girl? I don't know. That's the wrestling community's (decision). That's why you go to an NFHS rule book, that's why you look to see what other people are doing, that's why you take some time and plan and do it right."

The "do it right" that she spoke of includes having a classy experience for the participants, Berger said. Doing things the way the boys do them doesn't make it the best way for the girls, she said.

"To those who say, 'Just put a mat down at the boys' state tournament and let them wrestle,' well, what time? Six in the morning? Ten o'clock at night? What does it tell the young girls when you just sort of say, 'Go out and wrestle'? They deserve the same consideration and planning in a state championship as any other sport. I've gotta tell you, if you're going to build it, let's build it correctly so that it will last (a long time)."

If Charlotte Bailey's efforts are successful, more girls will get the opportunity to celebrate as Ali did—jumping into the arms of her coach—after winning a state championship at a tournament sanctioned by the IGHSAU.

Bailey is leading the charge to have girls' wrestling be a varsity sport and for girls to have their own state tourney. She was a gymnast in high school in Illinois, but Bailey got deeper into wrestling as her daughter, Jasmine, looked to improve already formidable skill in judo by wrestling at West High School in Iowa City.

"She wanted to wrestle so she could basically cross train her mat work, and then she tried freestyle and fell in love with it," Bailey said. "That pretty much changed everything for our family."

Jasmine Bailey became a four-time all-America wrestler at McKendree. Her mother became women's wrestling director for Iowa USA Wrestling as well as co-founder with her husband, George, of FEW—Female Elite Wrestling—a nonprofit that advanced the sport to some and introduced the sport to others who would have otherwise abstained because they did not want to wrestle boys. The FEW tournaments the Baileys put on were helped by Jenn Vetterick of Norwalk, who co-directed girls' state tournaments with Geno Hildreth at Des Moines North High School. Those tournaments flew the flag of the Michigan-based United States Girls Wrestling Association, which held the first tournament in Iowa in Gilbert in 2000.

Charlotte said one key sticking point in the spring of 2019 was that she and Berger differ on wrestling's place in the makeup of the state's residents. Charlotte said starting a girls' tournament under the auspices of the girls' union is a big deal.

"There's two layers to that. The first one is for people who understand the importance of wrestling in the culture of Iowa. The piece that says that's what we do here. The culture of Iowa says we wrestle, we work hard, and we embody the ethics and the principles that go into this oldest and greatest sport," Charlotte said. "Iowa is expected to be a leader in the sport of wrestling. No matter what other painting you do around the concept, Iowa is expected to be leading, so there's that piece.

"The second part is that sanctioning is a really interesting word to use because for a long time, that's what everybody was looking for: Everybody was looking to sanction the sport of wrestling for girls, and we spent twenty years getting the first six states to sanction the sport of wrestling for girls. Then last year, they stopped asking about sanctioning. Last year, people said wrestling is an existing sport in our state, we need a girls' division. When we quickly added a dozen states that have championship events as part of the high school season, the way that happened in most of those states is by recognizing that this is not a new sport, this is not an emerging sport, it's an existing sport that we want to grow and they just added a division."

Charlotte added, "It's really interesting that (Berger) doesn't buy Part A that I was just saying, which is that it's just our culture here, it's what we do. That's not a valid argument from her standpoint."

Berger responded, "The question isn't about whether we want to be a leader. The question is what sport right now do we want to offer—should it be wrestling? Should it be triathlon? I don't know, there are a lot of opportunities and, if you look at the fastest-growing girls' sports across the country, there's a lot of opportunities. It's not just girls' wrestling. I am trying to do what's best for girls."

Support for a second high school wrestling tournament each winter in Iowa is gathering steam in the state, Ali said. Her mother, Tonya, said it's a big deal in terms of a level mat for boys and girls.

"We have *a lot* of support because everybody is pushing for it. The girls on the team are getting their friends to go out for it, and the parents are supportive about it and not tearing them down, saying, 'No, that's a boy's sport,'" Ali said. "They're pushing them to get better because it not only betters you in life, it betters you in other sports and teaches you so many lessons that you'd never thought you'd get."

Tonya Gerbracht played softball at Wartburg College, where her future husband was an all-America wrestler and a member of the Knights' first NCAA Division III championship team. Tonya's brother, Jay Bollman, was a state qualifier for Waverly–Shell Rock. She sees a girls' wrestling tournament as being important. "I think it's a big deal in the fact it gives the girls an equal opportunity," Tonya said. "It's a great sport that teaches so much, so I think if anything that's a big deal. It allows those girls to participate because a lot of them won't do it because they don't want to wrestle the boys. There are so many things they can learn from wrestling."

Learning how to land the celebratory jump, for example.

"She hit me in the nose when she did it, but emotionally it was awesome," Chad said. "I've been coaching at AGWSR for twenty years and we've been close to getting a state champion, but it hasn't happened. So, it's kind of ironic it happens to be my daughter and this situation, girl against girl, rather than girl versus boy. It's a level playing field, so I was very, very happy."

Rachel Watters (*top*) never qualified for the state tournament while wrestling for Ballard High School in Huxley. She did win three age-group national freestyle championships, wrestled overseas on two world teams and qualified for the 2016 Olympic Trials during her high school days. *Photo by Dan McCool.*

Black said the Waverly tournament was big because it was an acknowledgement that the girls deserve their own tournament. "Yes, there are some girls' competitions, but without a final goal, what would these mean?" Black said. "Now the girls have one, they have a goal to reach, they have a state tournament. There is so much more growth that needs to happen. We can't be happy just because we have a tournament."

For girls' wrestling to grow, Charlotte said it needs a high school season.

"USGWA tournaments held before FEW did a great job generating excitement, giving the girls opportunities, but they were always opportunities that had to be pre-season or post-season and it only works for girls who had a parent willing to coach them because they didn't have a coach otherwise," Charlotte said. "A lot of these girls, if we assume that the majority of girls who wrestled in high school this year do not have a USA card, do not have an AAU card and do not have a club coach, then if the IWCOA doesn't put their tournament inside the high school season, the girls can't have a coach because coaches can't have contact with their athletes outside of the season (until June 1). That's why being part of school is important, because wrestling is strongest at the high school level inside schools, and we can't keep all of the opportunities for girls outside of when they have access to a coach."

Having girls on a high school wrestling team in Iowa is not as new as the twenty-first century. Dominique Smalley of Iowa City wrestled in junior high before competing at Iowa City's City High School. She said in a 1998 *Des Moines Register* interview the early workouts were awkward for the boys as well as for her.

"The guys were intimidated and scared of wrestling me at first, and I was scared," Smalley said. "Everybody learned to deal with it, just like you have to learn to deal with anything that happens in life."

Smalley won a gold medal in the 2000 FILA Junior Women's World Championships in France while wrestling for the Dave Schultz Wrestling Club.

Coaches may have been against the idea of girls on a wrestling team initially and took steps to make sure the girls would get no breaks in practice because of their gender. The respect was hard-earned.

"My experience of it was you had a girl like Jasmine or Cassy or, later, Rachel, who was just going to show up at practice, do everything the boys did and figure it out and just stay even if you weren't welcome there....When you had girls who were like that, they were not only successful on the mat, but they stayed. Then they turn around and they are competing for Team USA and competing at national events and doing really well," Charlotte said. "What I found was that there's probably a whole other group of girls who would value the sport, want to participate and do a lot of other things, all of the things we love wrestling for, but they didn't necessarily want to put up with being unwelcome....There was another group of girls where it wasn't worth it to them to give up some other sport, because most of them are multi-sport athletes, in order to have that experience."

What used to be considered a frivolous idea—girls wrestling boys in high school competition—has become much more accepted. Sluik told the *Des Moines Register* it was a matter of a willingness to put in the work: "Girls showing they can do it, pushing through practices, actually competing."

Black added, "Honestly, acceptance happens through growth I think. When people start benefitting from it or seeing it as a benefit, then they're willing to accept it."

The effort to find girls a niche in Iowa's high school wrestling landscape was further legitimized in January 2018 at the Upper Iowa Conference tournament. That's when Taylor achieved her unprecedented 100th career victory. She was a three-time conference champion.

Taylor decided to try wrestling after she was not selected for the cheerleading squad at her school. When she broached the idea of joining the team, Taylor said she was told making it through practice would be impossible.

"I started it because I had nothing to do…and then I (stayed) out with it because I loved it. Then that love turned into like obsession. I always wanted to be doing it," Taylor said. "When I was stressed and if I went and wrestled, I'd feel so much better about myself. It was such a huge stress reliever."

Berger said she's noticed how one-time foes of Title IX in relation to the sport of wrestling have changed their opinion in recent years. The government established an equal rights law, known as Title IX, in 1972.

"There was that time that college wrestling coaches were going to the Speaker of the House (at the time former wrestling coach Dennis Hastert) and trying to get Title IX thrown out because Title IX was killing wrestling," Berger said. "Interestingly enough, these same people are now calling for the addition of girls' wrestling."

Watters said she saw an example of how girls in wrestling are being accepted because of their work ethic by the boys at the Waverly tournament in 2019.

"It was probably the second match of the tournament, and there was a girl from Boone. I grew up in Ballard, and Boone was kind of our high school rival a little bit," Watters said. "There was a girl from Boone who won her match, and her whole boys' section, I could see them in the stands across from me. She won her first match, got her hand raised and all of the boys in the stands stood up and started clapping for her. I got this almost…I had to hold back tears. That was amazing. You wouldn't have seen that two years ago. It was amazing."

Charlotte said the girls' effort to be accepted in wrestling is like other attempts at seeking equality. "The hard part was that nobody wanted it to need to be that. The girls all thought the people would do it because it seemed like the right thing to do. They didn't expect to have to fight for it. I guess they thought we had come so far as a society that it only made sense that they could be there. The fact that it had to be a battle for so many of them, I think, that wasn't part of what they signed up for."

As she got her FEW tournaments started, Charlotte pushed the ideas of being classy and being in front of the crowd in selling the sport for females.

"Another piece that I did, and still do, is explain to girls that you may be the only image anyone has of a girl wrestler and, therefore, like it or not, you are an ambassador. People are judging everyone based on you, and it's not fair," Charlotte said. "If you're saying, 'Charlotte, you're holding me to a higher standard than the boys get held to,' I might say, 'Yes I am, but are higher standards a bad thing?' The idea for some of these little kids, I wanted them as ambassadors for the sport to look like you would look if you were representing the sport at the highest level, even if you were at a little kid tournament wasn't always comfortable. Not only was I pushing them to be persistent and to stand up for themselves and to work hard and to get up in tough situations, but then I was also pushing them a little bit to not just do what the boys do because the boys do it. I personally wouldn't mind if every tournament said, 'You'll wear your warmups to the podium,' and I don't think there should be a rule that says the girls have to do it this way and the boys have to do it that way."

Taylor, who was national runner-up in her first collegiate season at McKendree, was happy to see girls' wrestling in Iowa take a significant step forward in 2019, even though she graduated a year too early to compete in the event at Waverly.

Ali placed second in her sectional tournament and advanced to the district meet in 2019. Taylor's reasons to pay close attention to the district meet at Denver High School were twofold: One was her former South Winn teammates were there. The other was that Ali was competing.

"I knew she fell short. I know how she feels because I obviously did too," Taylor said, "but she has another year."

It helped the girls' cause that schools such as Denver, Waverly–Shell Rock, Osage and Charles City quickly put together girls' wrestling teams during

Wrestling is frequently a family affair in Iowa. In this case, Maddie Black gets some instruction from her sister Megan (*right*) while their brother, Tucker, stretches her out. Watching the action and observing the time out is their father, Matt Black (*plaid shirt*). *Photo by Dan McCool.*

the 2018–19 season. Waverly–Shell Rock won a girls' dual meet against Charles City, but that was not a first. Spencer and Gilbert had a meet in 2001, according to Dave Storm, who coached the Spencer squad that night.

Storm said he remembered Spencer won the meet 43–19, and there were twenty-five exhibition matches along with the eleven varsity bouts. Storm said a highlight of the meet was the presence of former Iowa State assistant coach Les Anderson, whom Storm said had a motivational chat with the athletes after the matches.

Spencer also played host to a girls-only tournament January 21, 2001, and the *Spencer Daily Reporter* account of the meet listed forty-three girls participating and representing eleven Iowa communities.

"Obviously, this year the numbers were able to help make that happen," Taylor said. "Previously we haven't had the numbers, so getting these girls to come out in big groups makes it a lot easier to be able to do these things. We're definitely taking steps in the right direction. I don't think it's going to be too long before they have a sanctioned girls' season and girls' state tournament, and it would be cool if we could get that along with the boys' (tournament). I was really excited for all those girls who got a shot to win a state title."

A History of Wrestling in Iowa

Having such an event in Iowa was likely unthinkable leading up to Groundhog Day in 1993, when Bibbs scored a 14–4 victory over Light inside Davenport Central's venerable gymnasium. Bibbs said in a 2019 interview she thought the match got too much attention.

"In my mind, I thought even building up to that match in the media that this is just wrestling," Bibbs said. "In my mind, who cares that we're two girls. Stacy and I wrestled against each other in youth tournaments as well, so in my mind I didn't understand the magnitude of why it was so publicized."

Bibbs said she changed a bit of her thinking in later years, when Charlotte contacted her about a contest during the 2015–16 season between McKinna Faulkenberry of OA-BCIG of Ida Grove and Brittney Shumate of Woodbine that was heralded as the first match of its kind in the state.

Three months after her match against Light, Bibbs became the first Iowan to win a women's freestyle National Open championship in Las Vegas. It was the first time the women's tournament was staged with the men's freestyle and the Greco-Roman events. Winning that meet gave her an opportunity to travel to Venezuela for the Pan American Games. That title in Vegas was a big deal, Bibbs said.

"It was, but at the same time all of that just happened so fast. It was women's freestyle, and I was always a folkstyle wrestler. I had a very short time to learn the basics of freestyle wrestling," Bibbs said. "I think it more so hit me in Venezuela. Because when you become part of the USA women's team and you meet up with them and fly with them, some were married and had children. It just blew my mind; I didn't think wrestling went that far—that people were doing it being married and after having kids—so I just had no idea that it was out there like that."

Bibbs is the daughter of former Davenport Central wrestling coach Melvin Bibbs. Her older brother, Tony, was a two-time state tournament qualifier for the Blue Devils. She participated in numerous sports growing up, such as judo, bicycle racing, basketball, soccer, softball and pee-wee football, as well as wrestling. Bibbs said her first wrestling match was in kindergarten.

In Iowa, girls played boys' soccer at some schools if there was no girls' program offered. There have been no official requests for boys to play girls' volleyball, since there is no male equivalent of that sport at the interscholastic level. If the IGHSAU sanctions girls' wrestling, Berger said her interpretation of the IHSAA's policy and of Title IX is that should a like sport be offered, a school would not have to allow a female to compete on the boys' team.

Some of the girls who made historic inroads in wrestling say having a girls' wrestling tournament is a big deal.

Rachel Watters: "I think it's so important because of all the lessons, all of the things I've learned through wrestling. I've come to the realization that I want to be a college coach, and that's what I really want to do with my life. It's something that is awesome, and I think about every day. I wouldn't have my future career that I want, I wouldn't be pursuing this career, I found (fiancé Evan Hansen) through wrestling. I am going to college because of wrestling; all of my friends are wrestlers. I owe a lot of things in my life to this sport. It's taught me so many things. It's shaped my personality. I've been doing this since I was a kid. It really does something to your personality when you get beat up every day and you keep getting up and doing it. I don't think we should shut that down for half of the population of schools."

Felicity Taylor: "Winning a state championship, that's big for anyone. It would be cool to get to that point, but then again it would be really cool for us to have our own sanctioned sport."

Megan Black: "It's a big deal because for so many years it's just been dominated by males. The best males in the world in wrestling have come from Iowa. Now, since they accept women on that same stage, that's huge. That's like saying, 'Yes, you deserve to get to wrestle as well and have those same feelings of accomplishment as the guys do.' It's a big deal because if it can be accepted here, it can be accepted anywhere."

Ali Gerbracht peppers her speech with various forms of the word *cool*. She said that state championship win was "super cool" and "really cool." She was just shy of being on a state championship softball team at AGWSR. Ali is a catcher on the softball team. The Waverly tournament was amazing, she said.

"Oh, it was just like, 'Oooh, I can't even believe this is happening,'" Ali said. "I'd always dreamed about it, but never thought it would be a reality."

After reality set in? "It feels super cool. I didn't think I'd be a state champion in anything, and here I am a state champion, so it's really cool."

The interest in wrestling for Ali has been nearly lifelong. "She idolized her dad, and he was all about wrestling, especially during the season," Tonya said. "She just wanted to go to practices because that's where he was all the time, so I just said, 'Just let her go. Let her go to practice, let her roll around. She might not even like it.'"

One reason mom was in favor of letting her daughter try wrestling, Ali said, was because of behavior. "I think most of the time she let me do it because I was kind of a stubborn child, so she kind of almost wanted to see me get smacked around a little bit. Maybe it was just payback," Ali said. There was an elementary tournament Ali signed up for, even though her dad was not pushing her to get involved. Mom tried to take her daughter to a mother-daughter basketball camp, but Ali did not like it.

"She would watch Iowa wrestling meets with her dad on the couch, [and] they're both screaming at the TV," Tonya said. "I could tell from an early age she just had a passion for the sport."

Ali paid attention to her pathmakers. Black was her idol. She wrestled Taylor.

"I used to have (Black's) picture on my wall when she got her hand raised at state. I put it on my wall and said, 'That's where I want to be. I want to be there, I want to be her,'" Ali said. "At Oklahoma nationals, she actually signed my picture, so that was cool. I wrestled (Taylor), and she's a great, great wrestler. It was good to be able to compete against her. She's definitely writing the story of her own."

Ali and Black had at least one competitive comparison. Black wanted to be the first girl to win a state championship against a boy, but Michaela Hutchison of Alaska achieved that status in 2006. Black cried when she learned of that accomplishment.

"It was kind of cool just to see a figure, but I wanted to be the figure myself," Ali said. "I was kind of pushing myself to be a better me and not idolizing somebody who had put in their own time."

Atina Bibbs continued a family connection to the sport.

"That had something to do with it, (dad) being a coach, and then my older brother, Tony, was also wrestling. He was three years older than I am," Atina said. "After school, my dad was the one who would have to watch me, so I was around the sport. I just asked him one day, 'I want to try it,' and it just took off from there. I was more just going to have fun. We were raised in sports, all kinds of sports, our whole childhood so it was just something that was fun and kept me busy."

Going to youth tournaments may have been enjoyable, but the reception she faced was not always that way for Atina. That's a change compared to today, where females in singlets are a familiar sight and the good ones have a following on social media.

"Looking back at it now, being a minority, not just as a female wrestler but also being biracial, there was a lot of things I had to go through that most others didn't," she said, adding she does not have firsthand knowledge of things being better now. "I really can't say because I haven't been to a youth tournament in gosh, so many years. Just from word of mouth and people

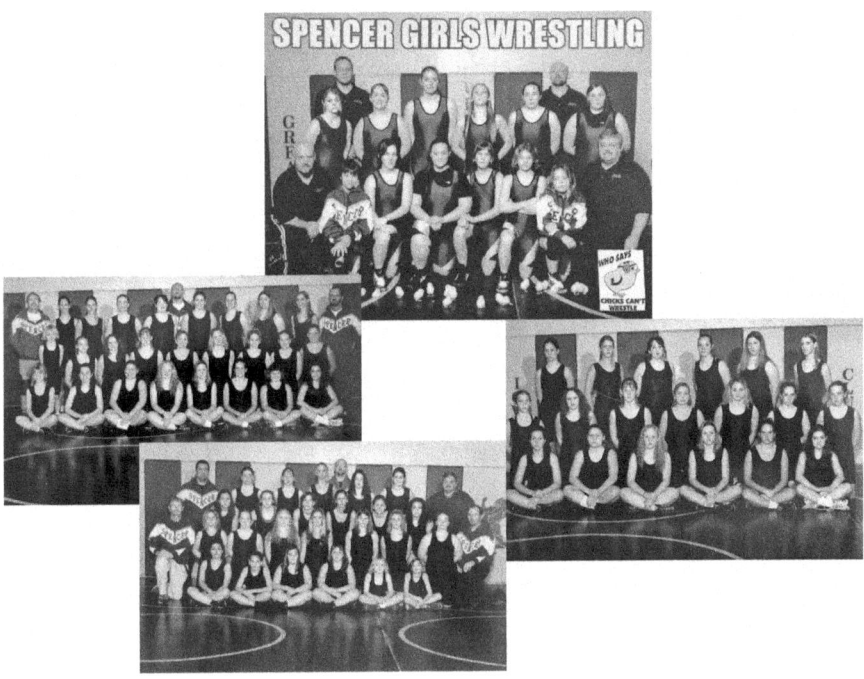

One of the earlier girls' wrestling teams in Iowa was from Spencer High School. The teams competed in numerous tournaments and also won a dual meet against Gilbert in 2001. *Courtesy of Dave Storm.*

that have sent messages saying, 'There's a girl here wrestling...' it seems like it's been more accepted. As times have changed, I think people have changed as well."

Why did she keep coming to the youth tournaments?

"The love of the sport. That's just what I grew up doing," Atina said. "I didn't see myself so much the difference in females and males wrestling. I just was a wrestler, so I didn't see things the way most people did."

Atina said she liked the one-on-one competition of wrestling and how her teammates were ahead of the game in accepting her as a teammate.

"I think what challenges you is you know it's going to be you on that mat with just one other person, and all of the hard work that you put in will shine," Atina said. "The team aspect is just amazing. The team I had in high school, they were so supportive. You had to earn your spot. You still had to do your battles and who came out on top got to participate in the wrestling meets."

Atina said her daughter was into soccer and volleyball, not wrestling, in high school. Had she chosen to wrestle as her mother did, the young lady might have had a touch of her grandmother Wendy Bibbs, who could announce her presence with authority.

"I would have backed her up and been her biggest supporter," Atina said, "just like my mom was. You could hear that woman from anywhere in a gymnasium."

The opportunities for high school girls to get some or all their college paid for by extending their wrestling career is appealing to many. Atina said she likely would have tried to do that if such an opportunity existed twenty-five years ago.

What does the future hold for girls' and women's wrestling in Iowa?

Berger hopes there is a unified voice in the how, when and where of a new sport.

"The instantaneous 'this is what I want' doesn't bode well for a systematic, analytical approach to adding something," Berger said. "I think it's true of anything that people are passionate about—universal health care, Medicare, IPERS. The way I want it is the way it should be done. I think you have to remove what is best for you personally and look at what is best for the sport and girls. It's a bigger umbrella picture and get together and formulate a plan—because you're all stronger together—and figure out how we're going to grow this."

By the time Taylor completes her collegiate eligibility, she said her return to Iowa could include several options for girls' wrestling.

"What I kind of would hope for them to do is make the seasons go alongside of each other or still give the girls an opportunity to compete in the (traditional) state," Taylor said. "Maybe make the girls' tournament that Sunday after state. If the girls would qualify for boys' state, they could wrestle the guys and then the next day they could have the girls' tournament. When they go to tournaments they could choose to compete against the guys. I think they should have the opportunity to wrestle guys if they want to, but obviously have that female option as well."

There are girls who watched Black or Herkelman or Watters and wanted to emulate their work on the mat. Taylor inspired several girls to hit the mat, and Ali is taking on that role of a teacher and an example.

"I love working with all of the junior high girls. It's so cool, the bond we've created," Ali said. "I was just sitting up in the stands, and some little girl asked to take a picture with me. That was super cool. She said she learns a new move every night since she saw my picture in the paper. It's just like, 'I never thought that would be a thing.'"

What if Ali woke up one morning and discovered the whole concept of a season of girls' wrestling and a girls' state tournament was a figment of her imagination? She'd rather not deal with that again.

"That's like how a lot of the girls' tournaments have been—they don't mean (anything) to anybody anywhere," Ali said. "It's almost like a slap in the face when you win those AAU tournaments and you don't get any support. This one, ooh, I'd be so mad if I found out it didn't matter towards anything."

Ali said she enjoys wrestling boys but finds a bout with a girl to be challenging. "These boys, they come out really physical, and the girls have a different build to them. (Girls are) not as upper-body strong, they can throw you with their hips. It's almost more intimidating to wrestle girls because you know what's at stake there, where (against) boys you've just got to go out there and take it to them. I have more to lose when I'm wrestling girls but when I'm wrestling boys I know that they think they can beat me, and I've just got to give it my all."

Maybe she was not predestined to make history, but Ali was going to be around the sport of wrestling after her mom initiated the idea of Ali going to youth wrestling practice.

Chad added, "Little did we know when she was that age that she would be in it for the long run."

News of Ali's championship spread throughout the state, fanned by the presence of newspapers and TV stations plus social media activity. Chad said increased media attention to girls' wrestling has helped the cause.

"There is a lot of media pushing this right now. That's the big thing—get the media out there, push these girls, celebrate these moments and good things are going to come," he said. "When she was eight years old, I thought by the time she was in fourth grade it would be a sanctioned sport, maybe a little further ahead."

Black said she is not a fan of most social media, but that aspect has helped grow awareness of the sport.

"I think you started to see a little turn of things and the girls were starting to get seen wrestling, and it was like, 'Wow, girls *can* wrestle,'" Black said. "Then you have different social media sites such as Flo and Trackwrestling that are now publicizing it. Not only do you hear about it now, but you can see it. I think that motivates people. As much as I don't necessarily love social media, I do think it had a huge part in growing women's wrestling because now you see those faces to the stories that you hear. You get to see girls out there scrapping just as hard as the guys."

A number of fans gave Ali a tip of the cap the following weekend when she competed in the North Iowa Cedar League tournament at Parkersburg.

"I kind of got that first taste of it. I didn't really know what to do. Everybody was like, 'Nice job, nice job, nice job,'" Ali said. "I kind of just tuned it out for the most part. I'm really grateful for all of them congratulating me, but most of the time I just go out and keep the same game plan, wrestle like I do and try to just stay true to who I am."

As her high school career nears one hundred wins, Ali said she is thinking about competing at the collegiate level.

"Initially, I think I wanted to be an orthodontist because I had braces on. (Now), it's honestly threw me in so many directions," Ali said. "I thought I had a plan to attend UNI, but now that Grand View is starting something up and I'm experiencing what I could do, I'm not really sure what I want to do anymore. At the beginning of the season, I was like, 'No, I don't want to (wrestle in college),' but with all these opportunities now and I've seen what I could do (wrestling) girls, I'm thinking maybe I will."

Watters looks forward to telling her grandchildren about the good old days of girls wrestling with boys as they attend a sanctioned state tournament in Iowa. Perhaps Ali Gerbracht, Megan Black and Felicity Taylor will get to do the same.

"I hope it's as mainstream as the boys' tournament is now," Watters said. "I hope that it's one of those things where you don't even think twice about it anymore. It's run alongside the boys' tournament, and it's not weird anymore, it's just there."

11

THE MALECEKS

A popular method for many high school coaches to build toughness and teamwork is to have a practice before the school day begins. That might be a series of hallway sprints and weightlifting, or it might be an opportunity for the squad members to roll around and get a sweat going to help ward off some weight.

That requires being at school by 6:00 a.m. or maybe 6:15. Being ready to go might require a 5:00 a.m. wakeup. In Iowa's winter months, you're getting to school before the sun rises, or perhaps you see the sun waking up. High school kids aren't fond of losing an hour or two of sleep. When you're done with school and practices, you go home in the dark to supper, homework and chores.

The Malecek brothers of Osage High School in northeast Iowa knew this drill. They could often be found checking their traps down by the river *before* it was time to get to the workout before school started.

"It just becomes a routine, it becomes part of your daily life," said Dennis Malecek, the middle of Joe and Marlys Malecek's three sons/farmhands. "Good habits or bad habits, you tend to stick with them. Fortunately, we picked up a few good habits that are part of our daily routine. I still get up at 4:20 every morning to work out. Every day. Five days a week."

Dave Malecek, the youngest of the three, spoke of two reasons why agriculture and wrestling fit like two soybeans in a pod. Dave started his thirteenth season as head coach of the wrestling program at University of Wisconsin-LaCrosse in the 2018–19 season.

A History of Wrestling in Iowa

There is a close tie to agriculture and wrestling among many families in Iowa. Dave Malecek is shown working for a pin for the Osage Green Devils. He learned hard work on the family's farm outside of Osage and later won two state championships. His brother Joe won a state championship and another brother, Dennis, was a qualifier. *Photo by Thom Bartels.*

"Number one, I think you just took more pride into it because it was hard work. Nothing was given to you. On the farm, nothing was simple," Dave said. "There was no fancy equipment—I'm talking the 70s and 80s and the early 90s—and you just had to put your nose down and go to work and you took pride in that.

"The second factor I talk about is the jump-in factor," Dave said. "I can tell right away who has grown up on a farm when we start moving wrestling mats because the guys that have just jump in. They don't ask questions; they just jump in and start working. You didn't get asked by my dad, 'Hey, do you want to help today?' You just jumped in from the time you woke up to the time you went to bed. You jumped in and helped out, whether it was gardening, whether it was picking sweet corn, whether it was picking up rocks, walking beans, baling hay. You just jumped in."

Lewie Curtis, wrestling coordinator for the Iowa High School Athletic Association, agreed on the idea that agriculture and wrestling seem to be joined at the stalk.

"It's a cornerstone or a foundation for so many people in Iowa, I think, that they do go hand in hand. I think too, wrestling is a sport that is all about getting your hands on things, pushing and pulling and manhandling things,"

Curtis said. "If you're a farmer, you've got to do the same thing, whether it's cattle or pigs or turkeys or whatever livestock you're raising or if it's just shoveling, moving things and pushing things around. That old-school way of doing things just lends itself to the sport too."

In regard to learning about toughness, that course was available at the farm, Joe said. "You get physical when you're sorting cattle and a 1,200-pound steer is coming at you and dad is yelling at you to not let the steer out," Joe said.

Dave said he got a kick out of one of his wrestlers bemoaning one aspect of a summer job. "We've got a guy on our team who is working on the golf course, and he's like, 'Oh my God, I've got to be there at 5:30,'" Dave said with a laugh. "I go, 'Awesome! On your way to work, call me because I'm already up having coffee.' I don't have to be at work at 5:30, but I'm up anyway. That's that farm kid mentality."

Dave also saw a more modern-day study of how farm life and wrestling can coexist handsomely while he was coaching. "Eric Twohey was from Stewartville, Minnesota, and wrestled for me, was a two-time all-American and now he's in his third year of medical school. You want to talk about hard work, that came right from the farm. I don't think he would have done a whole lot if he'd been a city kid, but he knew how to work."

When the Malecek brothers discovered wrestling, they found a way to do work without a shovel or a tractor. They were allowed to participate in two sports each year. The rest of the time was spent working on the farm. Football was a choice, but the Maleceks would often have a round of combining corn waiting after practice.

"We started sports, so we didn't have to stay home and work," said Joe Malecek, the oldest brother. "If we came home, we were going to get put to work, so hey, this sports thing seemed like fun. That was my motivation."

Joe said he learned a work ethic as he learned the sport of wrestling. "I'll tell you where I got my work ethic from. As a sixth, seventh and eighth grader going to these kids tournaments and never doing real well—I was tall and lanky and I wasn't that good of a wrestler—and to come home exhausted and to be told twenty minutes after you come home, 'Get your ass outside.' We had been wrestling at some little kids tournament all day on Saturday, but my dad had been home waiting for us boys to come home so we could work. There is nothing more draining mentally as a young teenager or a ten-, eleven-, twelve-year-old than being exhausted and being told, 'Now that you're home, you're going to start working.' We would have to pitch manure and help clean lots and all that stuff."

The work in practice did not afford too many extra sessions, Joe said, because the house was twelve to thirteen miles from school. There was work to be done at home, and there was an activity bus available. No one had time to drop what they were doing and run to town at any given time, he said.

Dennis said he learned early proficiency in hauling the device farmers call a "honey wagon."

"I remember being in second grade, I swear I was only eight years old. Dad loaded the manure spreader up, took the old 856 International out to the field," Dennis said. "He let me drive it out there and said, 'Pull the big shaft, the lever to turn the (power takeoff) on.' I did, and of course I could barely do it, and broke the drive chain right away. He didn't say a word, took it up to the shop, fixed the chain, back out there. (I) broke it again."

Dennis lost track of how many times he broke the chain.

"Within an hour, I had learned how to do that, and guess what? He had a kid that could now haul manure every Saturday between the cattle yard and the hog barn. To me, that was always the tie to wrestling because every time it became a routine: we'd haul manure, bed the shed, bed the hogs, do all the normal farm work and all of a sudden wrestling came along. It was like, 'Wait a minute. I can go to a tournament all day? Sit with my friends, wrestle a few matches and not have to haul manure?' It was the greatest thing in the world."

Was it fun? Was there learning?

Dennis: "To me it was. I loved the whole animal husbandry side of the business, the raising cattle and stuff. Today, I still have a few hobby cattle. I just love that side of it."

Joe: "Agriculture, especially in crop production, is very competitive just as it is in wrestling. In my situation, it was everything you accomplish is going to be you and everything you fail is going to be you."

Dave: "I think by my sophomore year it really kind of started making sense. This is what I need to do—it does go hand-in-hand. The harder I worked in wrestling or the harder I worked at home, it made everybody happy and you took pride in it."

Osage fans take pride in their wrestling team, known as the Green Devils. They have often enjoyed a bumper crop of wins in a season since the sport was introduced in the Mitchell County town during the 1930s. Osage has captured four dual-meet state championships and three traditional titles. During the season, the local newspaper *Mitchell County News Press* rarely puts out an edition without the Green Devils wrestlers on the front page.

Many Osage lineups, as well as some of the great teams such as Emmetsburg, Cresco and Britt, have been composed mostly of "farm boys" such as the Maleceks. All three Maleceks went to state in wrestling. Dave won two state championships, and Joe won one. Some of the "town boys" had names such as Schwab. In wrestling terms, Schwab is Iowaish for six state championships between brothers Mike, Mark and Doug. In 1985, Mark became the sixth Iowan to win four high school state championships, the best harvest an Iowa high school wrestler can reap.

The Malecek boys were graduating high school in the 1980s, when the farm crisis was anywhere from taking root to taking farms. Joe got a scholarship to University of Nebraska, got a degree in ag business and earned all-America honors in wrestling. Dave went to University of Northern Iowa, got a degree and all-America wrestling honors. Dennis played football at North Iowa Area Community College at Mason City and then turned his attention to engineering in college.

There were differing collegiate colors—scarlet and cream of Nebraska, purple and gold of Northern Iowa and blue and gold of NIACC—but as boys they were united in their love of Iowa State's cardinal and gold robes during the legendary meets between Iowa State and Iowa that were televised statewide on public television before the influx of cable and satellite channels.

"We grew up in the age of antennas, so on public TV would be the Iowa–Iowa State matches. We'd seriously as kids for Christmas would ask for (red) robes," Dennis said. "We wanted to look like the Iowa State wrestlers. I think we were all pretty much Iowa State fans up there, so we wanted to look like Iowa State."

It got wilder for Dennis as he grew in elementary school.

"I remember my sixth-grade teacher...and she was high school classmates with Mike Mann from Marshalltown. After that, I was just hooked. She knew Mike Mann personally? To me that was like knowing God."

Mann, a farm kid from Marshalltown, was a state champion before earning all-America honors four times—twice finishing runner-up—at Iowa State.

The IHSAA's Curtis, who led Underwood to a pair of individual state tournament team titles, said he noticed a difference between the farm kids and the town kids while growing up in Williamsburg. His father, Terry, was Williamsburg's wrestling coach as Lewie grew up.

"You always noticed that (farm kids) were a little bit stronger and definitely not afraid to mix it up, not afraid to get a little nasty if they needed to more so than maybe the town kids," Curtis said. "Even then, Williamsburg was a town small enough that a lot of the town kids still were maybe not farm but they were country-style kids, not necessarily a city kid that only walks on concrete."

While coaching, Curtis said he and his assistants tried to find the limits of the farm kids.

"We definitely pushed them as hard as we could. I think the thing that I maybe noticed with kids that were farm kids versus non was the farm kids, they very rarely, if ever, just gave in and wanted to go sit in the corner or had to visit the trash can in the corner," Curtis said. "They pretty much could just keep going and get through the hard times. The farm kids were always competitive and just wouldn't give in. Stubborn. They were stubborn in a way that they wouldn't give up, not stubborn in a bad way by any means."

Joe Malecek could have fit that description of stubborn when he was a senior in high school. He lost in the sectional tournament as a senior but managed to advance to the district meet—the table-setter for the state tournament—and then got to "The Barn" and won his state championship. Hanging out in the summer with friends such as Tim Krieger of Mason City or Royce Alger of Lisbon, two three-time state champions, and Osage teammates Mark Schwab, Glenn Barker and Brett Sweeney helped keep Joe's wish to succeed on high. The sectional loss made him up his daily mileage to six miles (sometimes with Schwab driving along and motivating him), and that was after school, practice or practices and a shift working at a grocery store. Then there was his coach, Bill Andrew. Gone were thoughts of anything but success.

"When you have Bill Andrew in the room, those kind of thoughts never come through your head," Joe said. "You just want to do better. I've had a lot of really tough coaches in my corner, and I still look back that the most motivational, inspirational coach I ever had was Bill Andrew. He was a lot like what I would envision his teammate, Dan Gable, was in high school. I don't know if (Bill and Dan's coach) Bob Siddens was that way, but Bill had a way of making kids believe they could do things they probably shouldn't be doing."

Joe said he's had no regrets about his time spent in agriculture and in wrestling. "Look at what happened to me, the accomplishments in high school, being able to wrestle in the summers, travel even though it was only Iowa. Doing well in the state tournament. I remember flying to Pittsburgh, Pennsylvania, and wrestling in the Pittsburgh Classic on Easter Sunday, getting the experience at the University of Nebraska, traveling the country, more than the wrestling the friendships and the camaraderie and the teammates. Guys are trying to make weight, it's 10:00 at night and you're in Chattanooga, Tennessee, in some gym. The camaraderie and the stories people have to tell. That's the kind of stuff you'll take to your grave. Farming is the same way. You've got some incredible neighbors who are always there. You work hard and they understand that. When times get tough, they're there for you."

On those days when school was called because of snow, a town kid might get some extra sleep and have a driveway to shovel or a neighbor with a snowblower. A kid named Malecek could expect some work and then a little fun.

"If we had a snow day, that probably meant the cattle bunks were full of snow and we'd have to go scoop them out," Dennis said. "That was back in the day when we used to get a lot of snow, back in the 70s and 80s, but we also got to ride snowmobiles too, so it wasn't all bad."

Joe said the work was often labor-intensive, but he remembered being able to have fun. "I still got to ride my dirt bike, I still got to hunt, fish and trap. I got to be a kid," he said.

The pride aspect that helped fuel his willingness to work in tough times followed Dave into coaching. He might have lacked that drive if he came from a different setting.

"There's been so many tough times. I think I would have thought more about money," Dave said. "I wouldn't want it any other way. I'm positive I don't think I would have had the same results. Even now as a coach, not having all of the resources I need, not having the best of the best. We talk about it all the time: Put your nose down and get to work, and everything's going to work out in your favor."

Dave said he wanted to win an NCAA championship in college. Don Briggs, then Northern Iowa's head coach, believed he could do it. So did assistants Joel Greenlee and Tim Krieger, Dave said. He said growing up in agriculture prepared him for the ups and downs that can come in a wrestling season or in a growing season. He saw his dad deal with it, and he'd seen his brother Joe do the same.

"I think of how he has had some ups and downs with farming," Dave said of his brother, "but by God he's back every year putting another crop in the ground. You keep going."

Today, Joe is a seed corn salesman and has a corporation that builds corn planters and sells tillage equipment. He also helps tend to the planting and harvesting on the land he grew up on.

Dave said his dad had some similar struggles. Dave likened his dad preparing for a bin-busting harvest that maybe didn't go right to losing a big wrestling match. "You've got to regroup and come back stronger the next time. He never gave up. That wasn't an option."

The farm in Iowa has the word *corporate*, not family, in front of it during recent years. Some believe the work ethic of the farm is eroding like precious topsoil. Participatory numbers are down in high school wrestling. It takes only a glance at the number of forfeits compared to actual matches to drive that point home. The number of family farms are dwindling because of the rise of corporate farming and the skyrocketing costs of trying to be an independent farmer.

"That's why some athletes fail at it, because it's hard. If it's hard, they don't want to do it," Dave said. "Not one part of it is easy, but the best part is to see what it turns you into. I think I would have been OK without wrestling, but I wouldn't have been very tough. I wouldn't have been able to make it through some tough times. Like when my dad died (in 1999), I wouldn't have made it through. I would have been a mess. Instead, wrestling made me tough and it taught me that good things happen when you work hard."

Joe added, "Times have changed. The tough farm kids of my era I think are gone. I'm sure there are some out there, but they don't exist like they used to."

Apparently, Dave's wrestlers at Wisconsin-LaCrosse have been working hard academically. He is proud of one harvest throughout his career: "I've been here thirteen years. I've had one guy not graduate. Every guy that wrestled for me for four years has graduated, and I take so much pride in that. I don't do it for recruiting purposes, I do it for my peace of mind, like this is my job. Will we win a national title? Yes. When? I don't know. We're going to keep doing good things and it's going to happen."

Dennis said he's seen the change in his business world: "Things are project-based. There are times you have to put in the fourteen-hour day at work seven days a week to get something done. Some people whine and moan and complain a little bit about 'get it done.' There's two kinds of people out in the world now. A couple wrestlers I've worked with through my career, they don't complain about it, they just get it done."

12
THE OTHER SIDE

Adam Allard seems to have a pin be the final step of each wrestling move he hits for West Sioux High School in Hawarden. Such a mindset has paid handsomely for the young man with black hair and a barrel of weaponry to be unleashed against opponents.

However, he may not be as well known to the fans of eastern Iowa as he is to the folks in most of the nine counties that hug the Missouri River as the state's western border. Hawarden is about a 250-mile journey from Des Moines, or roughly five times farther than if Allard was to drive 55 miles to Sioux Falls, South Dakota, to win state wrestling championships.

No wonder the geographic crack Lennis "Len" Liston said folks in the most northwestern part of Iowa make is more truth than trying to tickle the funny bone.

"We always said if the Big Sioux River ran a little farther east, we'd have been in South Dakota," said Liston, who was West Sioux's first state wrestling champion in 1967. "That's how close we were. You drive a mile out of my town (Hawarden), and you're in South Dakota."

Allard became the school's second champion in 2017—fifty years after Liston—when he took the Class 1-A 106-pound title. He has stayed in gold mode and will be seeking a fourth title in the 2020 state meet. Should Allard and Cael Happel of Lisbon in eastern Iowa be successful, they will become the twenty-eighth and twenty-ninth four-timers in tournament history. They will be equally remembered by the expected sellout crowd of between

A high school wrestler seeking a fourth state championship in Iowa often draws extra eyes to a weekend tournament. Alex Thomsen of Underwood and Brody Teske of Fort Dodge were both undefeated three-time champs going into their final season in the 2017–18 campaign. They wrestled each other twice—each wrestler won—before they collected their fourth gold medal. *Photo by Dan McCool.*

thirteen and fifteen thousand as well as those who keep tabs on those who have the most success during their four-year run.

"That would mean a lot," Allard said of winning a fourth championship. "It tells me how much work I put in and that it all paid off. I don't just work every day to come up short. I work hard every day, run every day, get conditioned every day. When I was (younger), we got these books and you could see all of the four-timers. I wanted to see my name on there. That's what I am working for, getting my fourth state title and being a part of the history of the state of Iowa."

Allard and Happel can further discuss being four-time state champions in college. Both are committed to wrestle at the University of Northern Iowa.

The western border gang had one of its better showings in the 2019 tournament. A total of fourteen finalists came from those nine river counties, and Allard and John Henrich of Akron-Westfield were two of five state champions. That was the most finalists since 2005, when sixteen wrestlers made it to Saturday night. There were six champions in 2005, a number matched in 2006 as the most since 2001, when ten championships were earned. The 2001 number was helped by Council Bluffs Lewis Central's record-breaking six champions in the Class 3-A tournament.

Jan George, a coach at Hinton High School, has been coaching in western and northwest Iowa for three decades. He said the sport can go through a roller coaster pattern through the years.

"It's kind of like mountains and valleys," George said. "You go up a mountain and you remember the days of Emmetsburg, Humboldt and Algona. Then you have Lewis Central, which goes on a big run, and you've got Glenwood down there that's pretty good. (Sioux City) Heelan had some good teams. Del Hughes (at Sioux City East) had some good teams.

"You look at West Sioux, they've kind of been up and down. (2019) is probably the best run they've ever had. Then you see what Ty Seaman started at (West Lyon) and the winning percentage there," George added. "Cherokee had some tough kids in the 70s. Emmetsburg kind of cast a shadow on everyone, but Cherokee had some tough kids—the Brad Smith, Gary Templeton and the Dave Storms of the world, the Karl Georges of the world. You get to eastern Iowa and you have that packed-in feeling. You get out here, and we're in the prairie. We have good kids, we just may not have that day-in, day-out competition like eastern Iowa has. We put some good kids on the mat, no doubt about it."

One sign of the western side's improving talent: Don Bosco of Gilbertville, a small-school power with eleven traditional state tournament team titles, travels 180 miles to compete in the two-day Herb Irgens Invitational at Ida Grove. That's one of the bigger regular-season tournaments in the state.

"Why do you think Don Bosco comes this way? They don't have to, but they want to because they want to know what we have over here," George said.

Allard and teammate/state champion Kory Van Oort helped West Sioux to a fifth-place finish in the 2019 traditional Class 1-A tournament after placing third in the dual-meet state event. Van Oort is the son of West Sioux coach Mark Van Oort, who brought a school-record eight qualifiers to the state meet.

"I think the main thing is more coaches that are not happy with the once-every-fifteen-years performance. The sport itself has changed, and I think that it's taken the western side a little longer to catch up," said Sergeant Bluff–Luton coach Clint Koedam. "We've all recognized the importance of off-season wrestling, the Freco series, camps, clinics, all that kind of stuff, but I think we got to resting on our laurels a little bit. I just think there are more coaches who are not happy with that, the one or two state champions in the history of their school, honestly just working a little harder to do the right things and encourage the kids the right way.

"For our school specifically, there was a day when we were happy being in the top twenty. Then we kind of bump that up to the top fifteen, then you bump it up to the top ten," Koedam added. "As much as we would all like to go from zero to one hundred from one season to the next, unfortunately it doesn't happen like that, it's kind of a slow and steady process. I think we've done better in the past several years."

Allard and Henrich have brought some welcome attention to wrestling in the western half of the state. Henrich won all 132 matches and three state championships in three seasons after his family moved from Rapid City, South Dakota, for the 2016–17 season. Allard lives in Akron but open enrolled to West Sioux. Through the 2019 tournament, the two had a combined 281-1 record in high school.

Henrich is a name synonymous with wrestling in Akron. Jim Henrich, John's grandfather, was the longtime wrestling coach at Akron and Akron-Westfield. Brad Henrich, John's father, was a two-time state qualifier. John was a two-time placewinner with a 93-36 record in three seasons at Rapid City Stevens (the high school that produced 1984 Olympic gold medalist Randy Lewis, a two-time NCAA champion at Iowa) by the time the family moved to Akron for John's sophomore season.

Some area fans might have done some digging to find his previous accomplishments on the mat. Others might have skipped that.

"Some people in town, it didn't matter that it was South Dakota, which fired me up," John said. "Some people were like, 'Yeah, whatever.' I didn't care. I knew what I was wrestling for. I knew what I wanted."

While he was busy winning, John made time to hang out with two cousins who are unable to wrestle or play football because of a blood condition known as hemophilia, where the individual's blood does not clot normally. There were numerous opponents who wished John would have been that cool guy rather than the guy who ruled Class 1-A's 160-pound division.

John's goal in the 2018–19 season was to be unscored upon. Mission accomplished, but he did not subscribe to the takedown–cut them loose–takedown approach if he could not score a fall. Often, one takedown was all John would tally in a bout. And it would not be a forced shot, rather a great set-up leading to another win.

"Every situation mattered," John said. "I never have (run scores up) really, and I doubt I ever will. That's just not me and not how I was raised by my coaches and by my family—to go out and embarrass someone. My coaches always taught me not to force stuff. That's one of the things I've been able to figure out is why would I try to force a shot that (isn't) there because it's obviously not going to work if I have to force it.

"I think that's one reason I don't get scored on a lot, because I don't take that many big risks," he added. "I'm not conservative, but when I push the pace, if I'm on my offense, it's hard for you to be on offense as well."

Henrich made an immediate impression on George. The bloodline was already familiar to George because he went to Northwestern College in Orange City with Brad.

"When I first saw (John)…I'd never seen him before, and after the first time I saw him, I said he had that look, that vision, that stare, kind of that (Brent) Metcalf look," George said. "His goal was not to let anyone score on him. You get some people who want to go takedown, let them up, takedown, let them up, but John's not that way. Akron's had a good program, and let's not fool ourselves. Mark Van Oort was the coach at Akron when you had some great wrestlers over there too. I think I was asked by a friend this year about John Henrich, and I just said, 'Make sure your kid has his shoestrings tied tight.'"

That sage advice could have been given to anyone at the Iowa state tournament who doubted John had the goods when he was a sophomore. An undefeated western Iowa guy? He'd wrestled in South Dakota? No one seemed concerned. John had two pins and won his last two matches by decision for the first forty-three of his Iowa wins.

"It made me want to wrestle so much more just to prove to the eastern side of Iowa that it doesn't matter what side you come from," John said. "It matters what kind of kid you are and how hard you work. Hopefully they learned that."

The lone loss was by Allard and came in the finals of his first high school tournament—his sixth varsity match. His 142-match winning streak includes a pin in 2017 as a sophomore over Blake Jackson of Millard South of Nebraska, in the finals of the Sergeant Bluff–Luton Invitational. Jackson beat Allard 3–0 in the finals of that tournament in 2016.

"I didn't really know the kid, but now I know the kid. It was a tough match," Allard said of the setback. "After the loss, I knew I just had to get my head straight. Next year came along, I had that kid again and knew I just had to stay more solid. I finished him off and wrestled really hard. I knew the time was going to come, I knew I was going to meet that kid again, and I got the job done."

Should he win the fourth title, Allard will have a side note similar to Mark Schwab of Osage, who became the sixth four-timer in 1985. Schwab had one loss in his career—4–3 to Dail Fellin of Mason City—and he avenged that loss with a similar score two seasons later.

Allard was on the smaller side as a freshman, but his strength and his drive were that of an upperclassman. Liston understood having a diminutive start to one's career. He was a freshman on West Sioux's first varsity team in the 1963–64 school year—there were twenty-four boys on the team—and he learned the value of conditioning from first-year coach Lyndon "Lyn" Dighton, who had just graduated from State College of Iowa in Cedar Falls and who could be found wearing a bright red blazer at meets and tournaments. Liston's brother, Allen, was also on the first West Sioux squad at 145 pounds.

"When I started wrestling…I only weighed eighty-four pounds and (was) about four-foot-ten," Liston said. "When (Dighton) started conditioning us, I told my brother, 'I think he's trying to kill me.' He would run us, and we had an old gymnasium that we had to practice in, and it had steps where the audience would sit. He made us run up and down those steps. We'd have three of us in a deal; two of us would be wrestling and the other one would have to run. Then after a minute or two, he'd rotate us, and you'd come down and wrestle and the next guy would run. He was quite a conditioner.

"There were probably two people that influenced me a lot as I grew in the sport. One was my older brother. He was a senior that year. When we went to sectionals, he got third and he was the one who did the best of any of us. The other was Coach Dighton, Lyn Dighton, and he influenced me a lot," Len said. "I just think the sport of wrestling was something that if you took it serious, it kind of went with you all through life, not just the sport, with the values, the individuality because when you go out there on that mat—which I tell some of the wrestlers from my high school now—that guy you're facing, he's going to want it just as bad as you do. Which one of you is going to get it?"

Len wrestled at ninety-five as a freshman and scored the program's first pin in fifty-eight seconds when West Sioux beat George 42–5 in the debut varsity meet on December 4, 1963. The *Hawarden Independent* newspaper account listed a small crowd, partly because of a lack of publicity, "However, spectator participation is expected to increase rapidly as this new high school sport—free of the ridiculous antics of television exhibitions—advances at West Sioux in an atmosphere of rugged competition."

That line about the size of the dog in the fight didn't work when Liston played football. "I went out for football in junior high, and some of the other guys who went out, they pretty much taught me that football wasn't my sport. I didn't weigh much more than the football did," he said.

Liston did not have a recent role model to emulate when he won his state championship. The closest winner to West Sioux at that time was heavyweight Del Perrin of Cherokee—roughly sixty-five miles from Hawarden—in 1942. After rallying for a victory over Paul Tonn of Jesup for the 112-pound championship, Liston remembered some post-match fun.

"I ran off the mat and jumped in Coach Dighton's arms," Liston said. "I don't think I thought of it that I was so much the first and only one to win a state champ from our area—it was that way—but probably when we drove home from Waterloo, about ten miles out from my high school they had a caravan of cars that escorted me back into town."

The *Hawarden Independent* report of Liston's championship said it was the talk of the town. Part of that was the semifinals match, where Liston avenged an 8–7 1966 tournament loss to Jerry Schropp of Cedar Rapids Prairie with a 5–4 decision. In the finals against Tonn, Liston trailed 4–1 late in the bout. He got an escape and a takedown to knot the score and then got the final margin to an 8–5 tally.

Liston, who lives in Rochester, Minnesota, said he'd like to make the trip to Des Moines to see Allard make history. Allard spoke of the two standing ovations the crowd proffers to a four-timer: one when the match ends and the other when he receives his fourth gold medal.

One state championship is nice, Allard said, but adding to that is better. "A lot of people think one state title, that's good. It is good, but if you can get multiple (titles), get multiple. That's how you know the kid is tough. It's not just, 'Oh, that kid had a good tournament.' He's dominated the whole season; he's done good every year. They know the kid's tough."

Allard said he can look at the list of four-time champions as a reason to work some more.

"When I see their name, I know they weren't just born good," Allard said. "They had to put work in, they had to put time in. I take time out of my day to work with my teammates. It all works toward that goal of yours, so I know if I want to be there I've got to get up, work when I don't want to work and put time in."

Koedam said building a program in an area where wrestling either has shallow roots or minimal success can be challenging to a coach in an unfamiliar role.

"Honestly, I kind of feel like a salesman sometimes where you've got to get used to rejections and you've got to get used to finding another way to skin that cat because that's what it boils down to. You've got to start with selling it within your team," Koedam added. "This idea that we've got to grow…five (qualifiers) is great, but when we only had one place winner out of those five, that (stinks). I'll never forget the year we qualified seven guys for the state tournament and had two place winners. I was embarrassed. Then you start selling the idea to your community, to your middle school kids, your youth programs and (bunches) of people are going to tell you 'No.' You smile, tell them 'thanks' and you keep trying. Now you branch out to that wrestling community in your area. We've had a lot of success working with other youth programs, bridging that gap of, 'I don't want to be with you, and you don't want to be with me because some recruiting might happen.' Let's get these kids together."

Koedam has enjoyed the perk of being a coach with a state champion—placing the ribbon and attached gold medal around the winner's neck on the awards podium—four times. He got to do it the first time in 2002 with Justin Bohlke of Kingsley-Pierson. The following year, he got to drape the medal on Brandon Bohlke, Justin's brother, and then got to award Colton McCrystal of Sergeant Bluff–Luton his treasure in 2012 and 2013. Getting to be a part of those moments is special, Koedam said.

"Addiction is a great way to sum that up. When I was younger, when I got to do that for the Bohlke kids there was a part of me that was like, 'Look at me, look at how great of a coach I am.' Now I would say it's grown to be a bigger thing than me. Fortunately, my maturity hopefully has grown enough, now you're putting that medal around that kid's head like a McCrystal, what goes through my head is all of the things that kid represents—the school, the community, his parents, our fans, our program. That black and orange being on that top step, it represents every coaching cliché word we can come up with—dedication, hard work, all of that kind of stuff—and the part that is so cool about that addiction is now you get addicted to using that kid as an example. Something I've been saying to my teams since McCrystal has been gone is, 'I want to start telling your stories' about a new kid. You can only say, 'Back when McCrystal was in school…' so many times before pretty soon Colton McCrystal is an old man and we can't be telling these stories anymore."

There is at least one more McCrystal story to tell. The former University of Nebraska wrestler won a gold medal in freestyle at the 2019 Pan American Games.

Koedam said coaches in the west are getting better at working together in off-season workouts. Workout opportunities have grown in Council Bluffs,

Sioux City, Underwood and Orange City. Koedam said there may have been a hesitancy in previous years about working with other programs.

"If we think we can grow our programs by being an island, we're all (crazy). I think the flavor that we're catching up to, that eastern Iowa has been on to for ten years, is you've got to have some different workout partners. You've got to be in front of other clinicians; you've got to have maybe some upper-level kids to train with in the off-season. They've been doing that for ten years. Hate to say it, but we're just figuring that out. I think something that is growing over here is you don't have to go at it alone. When spring rolls around, when summer rolls around, your own local program open mats are great, but there's getting to be more schools getting together, club formations."

John Henrich said he's not asking Grandpa Henrich for too much advice. They're busy teasing each other, but that has a purpose. John said he keeps a level head, the best thing he's taken from associating with the man.

The reality that Koedam tries to sell to kids is that any kid who walks into a practice room can be a McCrystal or an Allard or a Henrich and stand on the top step of the award stand at least once if he does the things necessary to get there.

"Not everybody is willing, but then that becomes our responsibility to continue to sell them on what it takes to be great," Koedam admitted. "I think the battle becomes what is the difference between do I spend my time trying to turn these kids into high-level performers or do I spend my time trying to turn them into good human beings? What I believe is it's not an option, it's both at the same time."

George said wrestlers from Woodbury Central, West Sioux, Lewis Central, Heelan, Sergeant Bluff–Luton and LeMars could make some serious noise from the western side of Iowa in the 2019–20 season.

"When you have certain people bring light to northwest Iowa wrestling or western Iowa, we all take pride in that," George said.

Koedam added, "I think we're going to see more individuals in that top-three category. I don't know when we'll have our next three-timer or next four-timer, but I do think those kids have had a great enough impact on this side that were kids looking, there were kids watching and paying attention and saying, 'I want to be that guy.'"

John Henrich will be at University of Nebraska when Allard starts his drive for four, and the other guys from the western border hope to have another big finish in Des Moines.

"We're starting to get some of the kids who have seen…let's say they have an older brother and the older brother didn't do very well, so they get back

A History of Wrestling in Iowa

The championship round of the Iowa high school state wrestling tournament cannot start before the 336 place winners do a ceremonial lap of the arena in front of a sold-out crowd. It's called the Grand March. *Photo by Dan McCool.*

in the room and are like, 'I don't want it to be like that,'" John said. "They put their head down to the grindstone and get to work. I think that's a lot of it, everyone is tired of people on the other side talking and talking and talking. I hope they keep putting their workout time in and showing up at state, let your ability show through."

Allard welcomes the opportunity to provide that light in his senior season, giving the kids someone to emulate.

"I want them to be like, 'Dang, dude, that kid's the real deal too,'" Allard said. "I want them to come up to me and get my autograph, take pictures with me. Whatever makes kids happy. They look up to me"

Some people on the verge of joining the four-timers list are hesitant to say much. The seemingly invincible Dan Gable even got beat, they might say. Cael Sanderson was undefeated in four seasons at Iowa State, but that was *Cael*—a generational wrestler. Allard stays focused.

"I don't overlook anybody. I know everybody's got skills," Allard said. "It's always going to be a brawl out there. I've just got to go out and work. I know if I work harder, it will show on the mat."

BIBLIOGRAPHY

Carlyle, Thomas. *On Heroes, Hero Worship and the Heroic in History*. London: Oxford University Press, 1968. First published 1841.
Cedar Rapids Gazette. "Ex-ISU Mat Star Now King of Push-Ups." August 21, 1979.
Chapman, Mike. "From Gotch to Gable." *Cedar Rapids Gazette*, December 27–29, 1978.
Davis, Mac. *100 Greatest Sports Heroes*. New York: Grosset & Dunalp, 1954.
Des Moines Register. "Mason City Girl Heavily Determined at 103." February 13, 2007.
Des Moines Sunday Register. "Brand Craves Olympic Gold." July 14, 1996.
———. "Not Your Ordinary Wrestlers." April 5, 1998.
———. "Title to Cyclones—Gable Fails!" March 29, 1970.
Fleischer, Nat. *From Milo to Londos.* Ring Athletic Library, 1936.
Hawarden Independent. "Liston Wins State Title at Waterloo Wrestling Tourney." March 2, 1967.
———. "Wrestling Emerges as New Sport at West Sioux Community High School." December 12, 1963.
Humboldt (IA) Independent. "Frank A. Gotch World's Champion." April 4, 1908.
Jefferson City (MO) Capital News. "Patten Rejects MU Post." April 18, 1974.
McCool, Dan. *Reach for the Stars: The Iowa High School State Wrestling Tournament*. Bloomington, IN: AuthorHouse, 2011.
Muscatine (IA) Journal. AP release. November 19, 1986.

Bibliography

Sisler, George. "Gotch Wins World's Wrestling Championship by Making 'Russian Lion' Quit." *Chicago Tribune*. April 4, 1908.

Smith, Russ. "Rule: Golf Is Mental Condition." *Waterloo Courier*, July 8, 1964.

Spencer Daily Reporter. "A Sign of the Times." January 23, 2001.

Taylor, Sec. "Caddock, Ex-Wrestling King, Dies." *Des Moines Tribune*, August 25, 1950.

Waterloo Courier. "Miller Ready for Challenge." November 10, 1991.

White, Maury. "Gable's Dream Turns to Gold." *Des Moines Register*, September 1, 1972.

ABOUT THE AUTHOR

Growing up in Clarion, Iowa, one learns of three things that make the area a special place to call home.

Clarion is the birthplace of the 4-H emblem, a four-leaf clover that reflects the group's pledge to use the head for clearer thinking, the heart for greater loyalty, hands for larger service and health for better living. The emblem was originally designed in 1907 by O.H. Benson, superintendent of schools in Wright County, of which Clarion is the county seat. The original three-leaf design was expanded to four a year later.

Some of the richest Grade A topsoil in the world is found in Wright County, which is the last of Iowa's ninety-nine counties. It was easy to determine your location by seeing the soil in a field: a robust black color means you're home.

Clarion is one of the state's charter schools that can claim having a high school wrestling program every year since 1921. There have been bright moments for some of the teams, known as "Cowboys" and "Cowgirls" through the years, but none share wrestling's limelight. The school has won the traditional state championship three times, won the dual-meet tournament once, boasts an Olympic gold medalist in Glen Brand and collegiate national champions in Les Anderson (NCAA Division I) and Jan

About the Author

Anderson (Junior College). The reputation has always been a team of tough individuals ready for an all-day fight.

The youngest of five boys, Dan McCool grew up in Clarion and never joined 4-H, but he is thankful for all the bounty coming from the rich farmland surrounding Clarion. He had one organized wrestling match—he got pinned—but always had a deep respect for the individuals who sacrificed fun, food and free time to have a chance at a gold medal. A fellow Clarion resident, Ray "Gus" Arnold, was a widely known wrestling writer whose knowledge of everything and everybody about wrestling made him someone McCool wanted to emulate.

Dan McCool embarked on a journalism career in 1978, spending considerable time covering the sport of wrestling. Through his coverage, McCool saw generations of individuals rise to the top, in part because many of them learned an appreciation for hard work on the family farm. It was hands-on stuff such as baling hay, shoveling and milking cows, and the occasional break gave them an opportunity to climb a rope. The calluses made tough skin, and the chores before dawn made backs unbreakable. McCool covered the sport from its youth level to the 1996 Olympics, working for newspapers in Iowa and North Dakota. His work earned him the "Bob Dellinger Award" in 1995 from *Amateur Wrestling News* and "Wrestling Journalist of the Year" in 1997 from *W.I.N.* magazine as the nation's top wrestling writer. McCool and his wife, Diane, who edits his work, live in Iowa with their dog, Frosty.

After leaving the newspaper business in 2009, McCool embarked on a career as an author. His first book, *Reach for the Stars: The Iowa High School State Wrestling Tournament*, was released in 2011. It has been updated twice and is in the process of another update in 2019. While waiting for the book release, McCool put together a listing of what is believed to be every individual who has competed in the state wrestling tournament since 1921 and the place winners at each weight. That publication, "Wrestlers, Clear the Mats…" has become popular for finding a school's wrestling history and for fans learning about their fathers and grandfathers, uncles or brothers.

He also provided writing assistance to longtime Iowa high school wrestling coach Bob Darrah, whose book, *Bobby D: "It's Not the Destination, It's the Journey. Ready? Wrestle"* came out in 2017. Darrah had a .950 winning percentage (340-17-2) despite having never wrestled at the high school or college level.

A History of Wrestling in Iowa: Growing Gold is McCool's first work for The History Press.

www.ingramcontent.com/pod-product-compliance
Lightning Source LLC
Chambersburg PA
CBHW040251170426
43191CB00018B/2370